Microsoft Office XP
EXCEL 2002

Copyright - Editions ENI - October 2001
ISBN: 2-7460-1361-4
Original edition: ISBN: 2-7460-1339-8

Editions ENI

BP 32125
44021 NANTES Cedex 1

Tél. : 02.51.80.15.15
Fax : 02.51.80.15.16

e-mail : editions@ediENI.com
http://www.editions-eni.com

Straight to the Point collection directed by Corinne HERVO

Foreword

The aim of this book is to let you find rapidly how to perform any task in the spreadsheet **Excel 2002**.

Each procedure is described in detail and illustrated so that you can put it into action easily.

The final pages are given over to an **index** of the topics covered and a set of **appendices**, which give details of shortcut keys and toolbars.

The typographic conventions used in this book are as follows:

Type faces used for specific purposes:	
bold	indicates the option to take in a menu or dialog box.
italic	is used for notes and comments.
Ctrl	represents a key from the keyboard; when two keys appear side by side, they should be pressed simultaneously.

Symbols indicating the content of a paragraph:	
▓	an action to carry out (activating an option, clicking with the mouse...).
⇨	a general comment on the command in question.
⌐🖰	a technique which involves the mouse.
⌂	a keyboard technique.
📄	a technique which uses options from the menus.

📖 OVERVIEW

📖 WORKBOOKS

📖 DATA

📖 CALCULATION

📖 PRESENTATION

📖 PRINTING

Microsoft Excel 2002

Microsoft Excel 2002

1.1 The Excel environment

A-Starting/leaving Excel 2002

▓ Click the **Start** button, move the mouse onto the **Programs** option and click **Microsoft Excel**.

▓ To leave:

File   Click the ⊠ button   Alt F4
Exit   in the application window

You may be prompted to save changes you have made in the documents which are open (the **Yes To All** option saves all open documents).

⇨ *If a shortcut has been created on your Desktop, double-click the Microsoft Excel icon to start the application.*

B-The workscreen

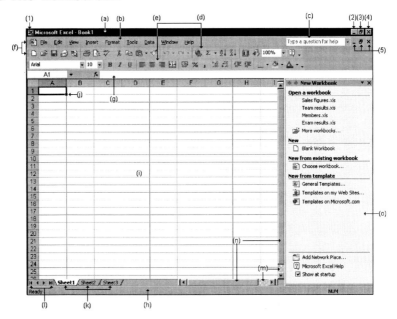

(a)   The title bar with the button for the **Control** menu (1), the **Minimize** (2), **Restore** (3) and **Close** (4) buttons.
                Below this, the **Minimize**, **Restore** and **Close** (5) buttons for the workbook appear.

(b)   The menu bar.

(c)   The **Ask a Question** text box, in which you can type questions or keywords to search the Excel help for.

(d) (e)	The **Standard** and **Formatting** toolbars.
(f)	Move handles: to undock a toolbar or menu bar, double-click its move handle.
(g)	The formula bar.
(h)	The status bar.
(i)	The workspace: a worksheet is made up of **cells**; the black square at the bottom right-hand corner of the active cell is called the **fill handle** (j).
(k)	The worksheet tabs: open a sheet in the workbook by clicking its tab.
(l)	The tab scroll bar.
(m)	The scroll bars: drag the **scroll box** (n) or click the arrows to move up and down or across the active worksheet.
(o)	The **task pane** is a separate window containing options relative to tasks such as creating new workbooks, finding text, inserting pictures and so on. By default the **New Workbook** task pane appears when you start the Excel application.

C-Using Excel menus

The Excel 2002 menus are special, in that they do not immediately display all the options. The standard options and the options last used will be the first ones displayed.

▓ To open a menu, click the menu name.

▓ To display all the options on the menu, open it then wait 5 seconds, or click ⌄.

▓ To close a menu, click outside it or press ⎋ twice.

⇨ *If you want to see all the menu options permanently, use the **Tools - Customize** command, select the **Options** tab and activate the **Always show full menus** check box.*

D-Using help

First method

▓ **Help - Microsoft Excel Help** or F1

*This command either opens the Microsoft Excel Help window or displays the Office Assistant. If the Office Assistant appears and you wish to deactivate it, click the **Options** button in the Assistant's yellow search box and, on the **Options** page, remove the tick from the **Use the Office Assistant** check box.*

*You can also show the help window by clicking the **Microsoft Excel Help** link at the bottom of the **New Workbook** task pane.*

▓ To show a list of topics that corresponds to a particular request, click the **Answer Wizard** tab.

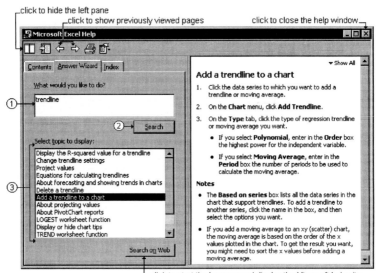

① Enter your question.

② Click to start the search.

③ Select the required topic to display the help text in the right-hand pane.

▓ To look for a help text using the **Index**, start by clicking the **Index** tab. In the **Type keywords** box, enter the first letters of the keyword you require then click the **Search** button. You can also double-click one of the suggested keywords displayed in the **Or choose keywords** list box. Select the help topic you require, to see its text in the right pane.

▓ To hide the left pane of the help window, containing the **Contents, Answer Wizard** and **Index** tabs, click the [▨] tool button. The [▨] tool button can be used if you wish to reopen this part of the window.

▓ The buttons on the left either arrange the help window and the application window in a tiled manner ([▥]) or place the help window over the application window ([▤]).

▓ To print the displayed help text, click the [🖶] tool button. Define the print settings in the **Print** dialog box then click **OK**. When you print a text displayed with the **Contents** tab, you will be asked if you wish to **Print the selected topic** or **Print the selected heading and all subtopics**. Make your choice and click **OK**.

Second method

You can also get help using the Ask a Question box.

▓ Click the **Ask a Question** box [Type a question for help ▾] on the right end of the menu bar, enter your question or a keyword and press [Enter] .

The topics corresponding to the search subject appear.

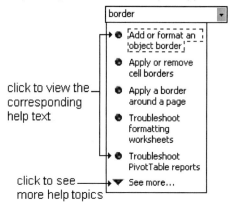

click to view the
corresponding
help text

click to see
more help topics

⇨ *You can also get help from the Office Assistant. Show the Assistant with the **Help - Show the Office Assistant** command, click the Assistant then enter your question or keyword in the text box. Click **Search** to start searching.*

⇨ *To hide the Office Assistant, use the **Help - Hide the Office Assistant** command or right-click the Assistant and choose **Hide**.*

⇨ *To deactivate the Assistant, use the **Help - Microsoft Excel Help** command (or F1) if the Assistant is hidden or click the Assistant if it is on the screen. Click the **Options** button, deactivate the **Use the Office Assistant** checkbox and click **OK**.*

E - Repeating your last action

▨ If necessary, select the object concerned.

▨ **Edit - Repeat** or Ctrl **Y**

F - Undoing your last action

▨ **Edit**
Undo

Ctrl **Z**

▨ To undo several of your last actions, click the down arrow on the tool button to open the list.

▨ Click the last action of the list you wish to undo.

⇨ *Excel 2002 allows you to cancel up to 16 of your last actions.*

⇨ *If you have undone an action, click* *to retrieve it.*

1.2 Managing what appears in the window

A-Managing the task pane

▒ To display the task pane, use the **View - Task Pane** command.
The task pane is anchored to the right of the application window.

▒ To change the contents of the task pane, click the ▼ tool button on the pane's title bar and choose the type of task pane you require.

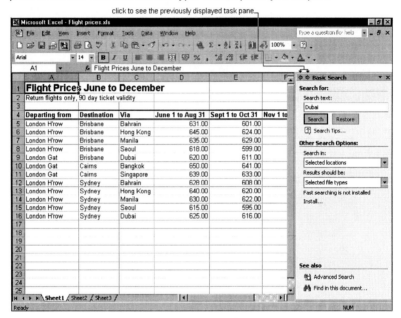

click to see the previously displayed task pane

Here, the task pane shows options for finding text.

▒ To undock (detach) the task pane, point to its title bar and drag it away from the side of the application window, or double-click its title bar. It then becomes a floating task pane.
To dock (or reattach) the task pane, double-click the pane's title bar or drag it by its title bar towards the right edge of the application window again.

▒ To close the task pane, use the **View - Task Pane** command again or click the ☒ button on the pane's title bar.

B-Freezing/unfreezing titles on the screen

▒ Click inside the column which follows the row titles you want to freeze, and/or click inside the row which comes after the column titles.

▒ **Window - Freeze Panes**

⇨ *To release the titles you have frozen use **Window - Unfreeze Panes**.*

⇨ *You can also display two different parts of the worksheet simultaneously by splitting the window. To do this, drag the split bar located at the top of the vertical scroll bar* 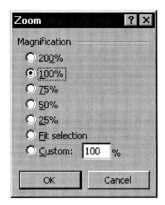 *and/or the split bar located at the right end of the horizontal scroll bar* , *depending on whether you want to split horizontally or vertically. This action produces two separate panes, each of which can display a different area of rows and/or columns, allowing you to work on two distant parts of the same worksheet. To remove the split, use the* **Window - Remove Split** *command.*

C-Zooming in on the workspace

▓ View - Zoom

⇨ *The zoom scale can also be chosen from the list on the* **Standard** *tool-bar.*

⇨ *To fit the worksheet to the size of the screen, use the command* **View - Full Screen**.

D-Hiding/displaying zero values

▓ Tools - Options - View tab

▓ In the **Window options** frame, deactivate (or activate) the **Zero values** option.

⇨ *To hide zero values in selected cells only, apply a custom format (0;0;) to the cells.*

E-Displaying values in Euros or another currency

▓ If necessary, display the **EuroValue** toolbar with the **View - Toolbars - EuroValue** command.

*If the toolbar is unavailable, the corresponding add-in has not been loaded. To load it, choose **Euro Currency Tools** in the **Add-Ins** available list (**Tools - Add-Ins**). If the add-in does not appear in the list, click the **Browse** button to find it and load it. If a message appears to advise you that the component is not installed, insert the Excel 2002 or Office XP CD-ROM, if necessary, and click **Yes** to install the required component.*

▓ Open the 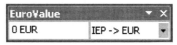 list on the **EuroValue** toolbar to select the type of conversion required, from a currency into Euros or from Euros into another currency.

The above example shows how to convert Irish pounds (punts) into Euros.

ISO Code	Currency Unit
ATS	Schilling (Austria)
BEF	Franc (Belgium)
DEM	Deutschmark (Germany)
ESP	Peseta (Spain)
FIM	Markka (Finland)
FRF	Franc (France)
IEP	Punt (Ireland)
ITL	Lira (Italy)
LUF	Franc (Luxembourg)
NLG	Guilder (Netherlands)
PTE	Escudo (Portugal)
EUR	Euro (Member states of the euro zone)

▓ To convert a cell value and display the result in the first box on the **EuroValue** toolbar, click that cell.

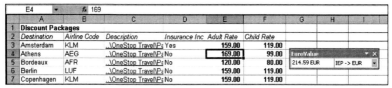

▓ To show the converted sum of the values of a range, select that range of cells.

F- Displaying the results of a calculation on the status bar

░ Select the cells involved in the calculation.
░ Right-click the status bar where **Sum** appears.

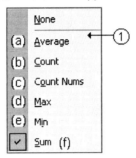

① Click the appropriate function:

(a)   to display the average value of the selected cells.

(b)   to display the number of alphanumerical or numerical values in the selection.

(c)   to display the number of numerical values in the selection.

(d)   to display the greatest value in the selection.

(e)   to display the smallest value in the selection.

(f)   to display the total of the values in the cells.

G- Displaying formulas instead of values

░ **Tools - Options - View** tab
░ Activate the **Formulas** option under **Window Options**.

H- Unhiding/hiding an open workbook

░ To display a hidden workbook, click that workbook's button on the taskbar.
░ To hide a workbook, activate another workbook or use **Window - Hide** to hide the active workbook.

I- Docking/undocking a toolbar

░ To dock a floating bar, double-click the title bar.
░ To undock a toolbar, double-click its move handle: it becomes a floating toolbar.

J- Displaying/hiding a specific toolbar

▓ Right-click any toolbar:

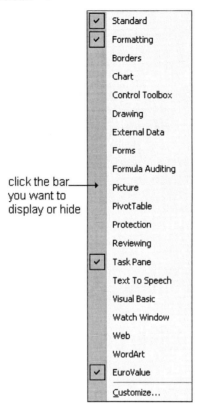

✓	Standard
✓	Formatting
	Borders
	Chart
	Control Toolbox
	Drawing
	External Data
	Forms
	Formula Auditing
	Picture
	PivotTable
	Protection
	Reviewing
✓	Task Pane
	Text To Speech
	Visual Basic
	Watch Window
	Web
	WordArt
✓	EuroValue
	Customize...

click the bar you want to display or hide

▓ To display several toolbars at once, click **Customize** and select them in the list under the **Toolbars** tab.

⇨ *Click* [▨] *on the **Standard** toolbar to display or hide the **Drawing** toolbar.*

K-Creating a custom toolbar

▓ **View - Toolbars - Customize - Toolbars** tab
▓ Click the **New** button.
▓ Give a name for the toolbar, then enter.
  A toolbar appears on the worksheet: it has no tools yet.
▓ To construct the new toolbar, activate the **Commands** tab then drag the required options from the **Commands** list onto the new toolbar.
▓ When all the buttons have been added to the toolbar, click **Close**.

L-Managing tools in a toolbar on the screen

Removing a button from a toolbar

▧ **View - Toolbars - Customize**

▧ Drag the button to be deleted away from any bar or menu and close the dialog box.

Adding a tool button or a menu

▧ **View - Toolbars - Customize**

▧ Click the **Commands** tab.

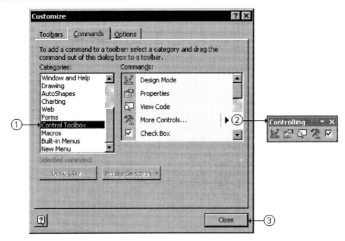

① Select the tool's category to add a tool button, or select **Built-in Menus** to add a menu.

② Drag the command or the menu from the dialog box onto the toolbar or the menu bar.

③ Close the dialog box.

⇨ *Once a toolbar has been customised, you can restore the original version by clicking the **Reset** button in the **Customize** dialog box (**Toolbars** tab).*

⇨ *On the extreme right of some toolbars, there is a* ▣ *button which you can click to add or remove tool buttons or menus.*

⇨ *To move a tool button within a toolbar, simply drag the tool button concerned to its new position.*

M- Customising menus

▧ **Tools - Customize - Commands** tab

▧ To add a new menu, select the **New Menu** option in the **Categories** pane then select the **New Menu** option in the **Commands** pane and drag it to the required position on the menu bar. Use the **Modify Selection** button to give a name to your menu.

- To add an option to a menu, open the menu concerned in the menu bar. Under the **Commands** tab of the **Customize** dialog box, select the required option in the **Categories** list. Select the option you wish to add in the **Commands** pane and drag it onto the menu that you opened.

- To rename a menu or a menu option, in the menu bar select the menu or the menu option concerned. Under the **Commands** tab of the **Customize** dialog box click the **Modify Selection** button then change the **Name**. Enter the **&** character immediately before the letter that must appear underlined.

- To delete a menu or a menu option, select the menu or the menu option concerned in the menu bar and drag it clear of any menu or toolbar.

- When you have finished customising your menus, click the **Close** button on the **Customize** dialog box.

1.3 Moving around/selecting in a worksheet

A-Moving around in a sheet

⌐ Use the scroll bars:

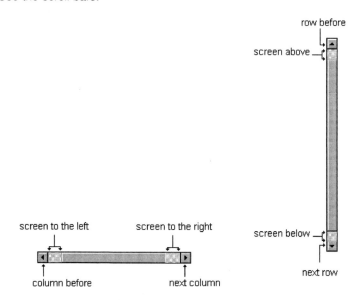

row before

screen above

screen to the left   screen to the right   screen below

column before   next column   next row

⇨ *As you drag the scroll box, Excel displays the row number or the column letter in a ScreenTip.*

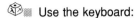 Use the keyboard:

cell to the right/to the left	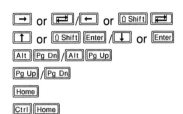
cell above/below	
screen to the right/to the left	
screen above/below	
column A in the active row	
cell A1	

⇨ *To reach a specific cell, select the reference of the active cell on the formula bar and enter the reference of the cell where you want to go.*

B-Finding a cell

By its contents

▓ If you want to search the whole sheet, activate cell A1, otherwise select the range concerned.

▓ **Edit - Find** or ⌷Ctrl⌷ **F**

▓ Enter the value you want to find, activate the appropriate options to indicate how to carry out the search, then confirm.

▓ To search cell by cell, click the **Find Next** button. If the cell found contains what you were looking for, click the **Close** button; if not, click **Find Next** to keep searching.

▓ To search all cells simultaneously, click the **Find All** button. When you do this, a detailed list of the cells found appears in the bottom part of the dialog box.

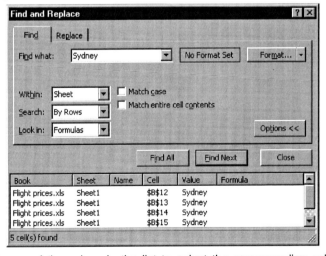

▓ Click one of the values in the list to select the corresponding cell. Click the **Close** button.

By its formatting

▓ Activate a single cell or select the part of the sheet in which you want to search.

▓ **Edit - Find** or Ctrl **F**

▓ If necessary, click the **Options** button to show the full range of search options.

▓ Delete anything that may be still in the **Find what** box.

▓ Click the **Format** button and in the **Find Format** dialog box, select the options for the required format.

The Choose Format From Cell button automatically retrieves all of the selected cell's formatting attributes.

▓ Click **OK**.

C-Moving from one sheet to another

▓ Using the tab scroll buttons, display the name of the sheet to which you want to go. Click the tab to activate the sheet.

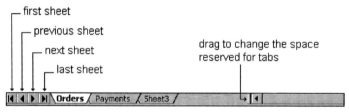

first sheet
previous sheet
next sheet
last sheet
drag to change the space reserved for tabs

⇨ *To scroll the tabs quickly, keep the* ⇧ Shift *key pressed down while clicking* ◀ *or* ▶.

⇨ *On the keyboard you can use* Ctrl Pg Dn *to move to the next sheet or* Ctrl Pg Up *for the previous sheet.*

⇨ *You can move the sheet to a different position in the workbook by dragging its tab.*

D-Selecting a range of adjoining cells

▓ This can be done in three ways:

Dragging	Click the first cell of the selection and drag over the others. When you are satisfied with the selection, release the mouse button.
⇧ Shift -clicking	Click the first cell to be selected and then point to the last one. Hold down ⇧ Shift then click at the same time. Release the mouse button before the ⇧ Shift key.
On the keyboard	Hold down the ⇧ Shift key and use the direction keys.

Microsoft Excel 2002

E-Selecting non-adjacent cells

▓ Select the first cell/range of cells.

▓ Point to the first cell of the next range then press the [Ctrl] key and drag, if necessary, to select a range of cells.

▓ Release the [Ctrl] key.

⇨ *In a formula or a dialog box, selected ranges which are non-adjacent are separated by a comma. For example: A5:A10,L5:L10 refers to the ranges of A5 to A10 and L5 to L10.*

F-Selecting rows and columns

▓ The following methods can be used:

	Row	**Column**
🖱	Click the row number.	Click the column letter.
🎲	Activate a cell in the row and press [⇧ Shift] [space].	Activate a cell in the column and press [Ctrl] [space].

⇨ *To select several rows (or columns) at a time, you can drag over them, or hold down [⇧ Shift] and click.*

⇨ *To select the entire worksheet, click the button in the top left corner, where the column containing row numbers meets the row containing column letters or press [Ctrl] [⇧ Shift] [space] or [Ctrl]* **A.**

G-Selecting cells according to content

▓ **Edit - Go To** or [F5] or [Ctrl] **G**

▓ Click the **Special** button.

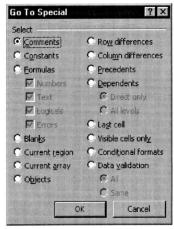

▓ Indicate the type of cells to be selected.

2.1 Managing workbooks

A-Opening a workbook

▓ **File**
   Open

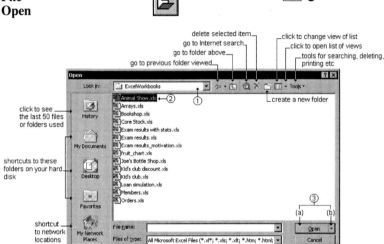

① Open the folder containing the document.

② Select the document.

③ Choose:

   (a)   to open the document normally.

   (b)   to open the document as read-only, as a copy, in a browser, or to repair it.

▷ *You can open several documents at once: use the* Ctrl *and/or* ⇧ Shift
   keys to select them first.

▷ *The names of the last four documents appear at the end of the* **File**
   menu: click one of them to open the document.

B-Saving a document

A new document

▓ **File**
   Save

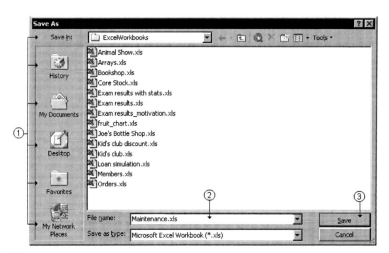

① Activate the disk and the folder where the document is to be saved.

② Give the document's name (up to 255 characters, including spaces).

③ Save the document.

⇨ *Excel documents have the extension .XLS (this may be hidden, according to the view options of your Windows Explorer).*

Existing documents

▓ File   Ctrl S
Save

⇨ *To update the summary of a document, use **File - Properties** and fill in the **Summary** page.*

C-Activating AutoRecover

If you have a technical problem such as a power cut or an application failure, Excel can help you to recover a lost file, in most cases. However, to allow Excel to do this, you must have activated the AutoRecover feature before the incident occurs.

▓ Tools - Options - Save tab

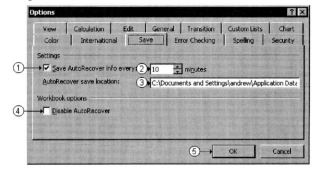

① Make sure this option is activated.

② Specify the time interval between two saves of AutoRecover information.

③ If necessary, modify the location in which you want Excel to save the AutoRecover information.

④ Make sure this option is not activated so that Excel will be able to recover data in the event of a problem.

⑤ Click to confirm.

⇨ *You must never consider the AutoRecover feature as a substitute for regularly saving your work.*

D-Recovering data lost after a technical incident

*When you reopen the Excel application following a technical incident such as a power cut or the failure of an application, the **Document Reco-very** pane appears automatically to allow you to recover the files that were open when the incident occurred.*

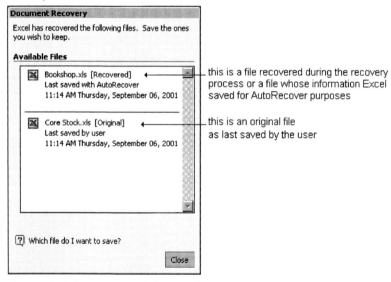

Document Recovery

Excel has recovered the following files. Save the ones you wish to keep.

Available Files

Bookshop.xls [Recovered]
Last saved with AutoRecover
11:14 AM Thursday, September 06, 2001

this is a file recovered during the recovery process or a file whose information Excel saved for AutoRecover purposes

Core Stock.xls [Original]
Last saved by user
11:14 AM Thursday, September 06, 2001

this is an original file as last saved by the user

Which file do I want to save?

Close

▦ For eachof the recovered files, point to the file name, open the associated drop-down list and choose to **Open, Save As** or **Show Repairs**.

If you click the name of the recovered file directly, it will open by default.

▦ If you want to save the version proposed, save the workbook. Otherwise, close the workbook without saving it.

*When you have dealt with all the recovered files, the **Document Recovery** pane closes automatically.*

WORKBOOKS

E-Choosing the default file location

▓ Tools - Options - General tab

specifies the folder →
proposed by default

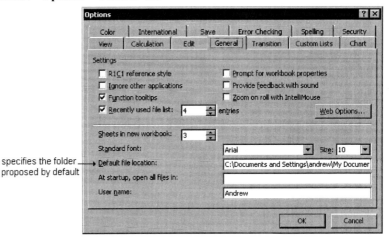

F-Closing workbooks

| ▓ File Close | Click ☒ in the workbook window | Ctrl F4 or Ctrl W |

▓ Save the workbook, if appropriate.

▷ *To close all open workbooks, hold down the* ⬆ Shift *key as you open the* File *menu then click Close All.*

G-Creating a new workbook

| ▓ File New | | Ctrl N |

▓ Click the **Blank Workbook** link in the **New Workbook** task pane.

H-Creating a workbook based on a template

▓ If necessary, use the **File - New** command to show the **New Workbook** task pane.

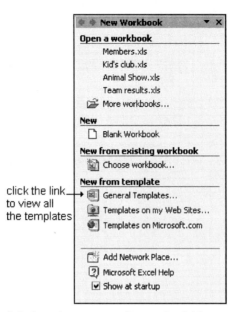

click the link
to view all
the templates

- If necessary, click the tab corresponding to the folder containing the template, then double-click the icon representing the template.
- Enter the information you wish into the new workbook then save this new workbook as you would save any other.

⇨ *When you have created a workbook from a template, the template's name appears as a link in the New from template section on the New Workbook task pane. You can now click the link to create a new workbook based on that template.*

⇨ *The Templates on my Web Sites and Templates on Microsoft.com links in the New from template section on the New Workbook task pane take you to Web sites so you can download other templates.*

⇨ *If you decide to create a workbook based on a predefined Excel template, you may see a message telling you that the corresponding component is not installed. If this happens, insert the installation CD-ROM into the drive and click Yes to install the component.*

I- Creating a workbook from an existing one

- If necessary, use the **File - New** command to show the **New Workbook** task pane.
- Click the **Choose workbook** link in the **New from existing workbook** section.
- Select the workbook of your choice, then click the **Create New** button.

  Excel opens a copy of the chosen workbook, giving it the same name followed by a number.

- Save this workbook as you would save any other.

J- Establishing a hyperlink with another document

▓ Select the cell in which you want the link to appear.

▓ **Insert**
Hyperlink

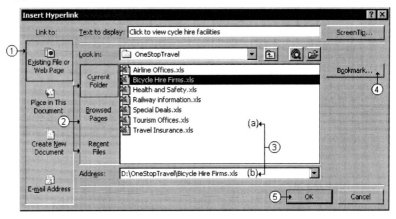

① Activate this icon.

② Activate one of these three shortcuts according to the location of the document to which you want to set up your hyperlink.

③ Select the file (a) to which you want to set up you hyperlink or enter its access path directly (b).

This document can reside on you hard disk, on your local network or at an Internet address.

④ To go straight to a specific point in the workbook, click this button then select or enter the name of the item you want to reach.

You can use a cell reference, the name of a worksheet or a named range of cells etc.

⑤ Click to create the link.

	A	B	C	D	E
1	Last year's sales figures				
2					
3		Books	Music	IT	Other
4	WEST	1100	1300	1550	1500
5	SOUTH	890	1200	1250	1260
6	NORTH	1250	1650	1600	1850
7	EAST	550	750	1080	1000
8	Average	947.5	1225	1370	1402.5
9	Total	3790	4900	5480	5610
10					
11	Results for each team				
12					

└a click on the hyperlink opens the document

⇨ *To delete the link, click it and hold down the mouse button for a few seconds so that you select the cell (if you simply click the link you will activate it) then press the* Del *button.*

K-Finding files, items or Web pages

Carrying out a basic search

You can search for the names of files or items or for specific text within them. From Excel 2002 you can search for Office files (made with Excel, Word, PowerPoint or Access), Outlook items (messages, contacts, tasks) or Web pages.

Click the ▣ button on the **Standard** toolbar to open the **Basic Search** task pane.

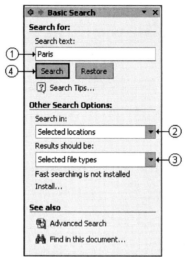

① Enter the required text.

② Specify where the search should be carried out, by using this list or by entering the file path for the search location.

③ Specify the type of files you want to find.

④ Click to start the search.

You may see a message telling you that the corresponding component is not installed. If this happens, insert the installation CD-ROM and click Yes to install the component.

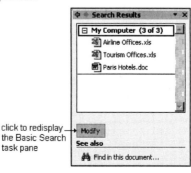

click to redisplay the Basic Search task pane

*If you wish to interrupt the search in progress, click the **Stop** button at the bottom of the task pane. If you stop a search or the search is complete, the **Modify** button appears instead.*

To open one of the items found (a file, Web page or Outlook item), click its name.

To display the shortcut menu associated with one of the items found, point to the item then click the arrow which appears. The options in the shortcut menu allow you to open the item in its application, create a new item from that one, copy the link into the clipboard or show its properties.

When you have finished all your searches, you can close the task pane by clicking its ⊠ button or deactivating the 🔁 tool.

⇨ *The options within the **Basic Search** task pane can also be found under the **Basic** tab in the **Search** dialog box (**File - Open**, open the **Tools** list and click the **Search** option).*

Carrying out an advanced search

Click the 🔁 button on the **Standard** toolbar then click the **Advanced Search** link.

To set each search criteria:

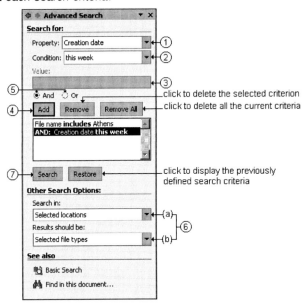

① Open the list and select the characteristic to include in the search.
② Set the search condition.
③ If required, enter a comparative value.
④ Click to add the defined criterion.

⑤ If you wish to set another condition, select an operator: **And** if all the conditions must be met simultaneously or **Or** if one or the other can be met.

⑥ Define where the search should be carried out (a) and indicate the type of items sought (b).

⑦ Click to start the search.

*You may see a message telling you that the corresponding component is not installed. If this happens, insert the Excel 2002 or Office XP CD-ROM into the drive and click **Yes** to install the component.*

*The list of items found appears gradually in the **Search Results** task pane.*

*If you wish to interrupt the search in progress, click the **Stop** button at the bottom of the task pane. If you stop a search or the search is complete, the **Modify** button appears instead.*

▓ When you have finished all your searches, you can close the task pane by clicking its ☒ button or deactivating the 🔳 tool button.

⇨ *The options within the **Advanced Search** task pane can also be found under the **Advanced** tab in the **Search** dialog box (**File** - **Open**, open the **Tools** list and click the **Search** option).*

L-Using e-mail

Sending a worksheet as the body of a mail message

This technique allows the recipient to read data produced with Excel, even if he/she does not have the application installed on his/her computer.

▓ Open the workbook then activate the sheet you want to send.

▓ **File** - **Send To** - **Mail Recipient** or 🖫

*The first time you use this command, a dialog box appears and prompts you to specify if you want to **Send the entire workbook as an attachment** or **Send the current sheet as the message body**. You should choose the second option.*

_click to close the e-mail window without sending the message

This screen may differ depending on the e-mail software used by default.

① Indicate the e-mail address(es) of the recipient(s) (b) by typing them in (use a semi-colon to separate each address from the next) or by selecting them from an address book (a).

② If necessary, indicate any addresses to which you want to send a carbon copy of the message, using an address book (a) or by entering them directly (b).

③ If necessary, change the message title.

④ If necessary, enter a comment.

⑤ Click to send a copy of the active worksheet to the mail recipient(s). This sheet will make up the body of the message.

Sending a worksheet as an attached file

Using this method requires that the recipient already has Excel installed on his/her computer.

░ Open or create the worksheet you want to send.

You can send only a whole worksheet and not a part of one.

░ **File - Send to - Mail Recipient (as Attachment)**

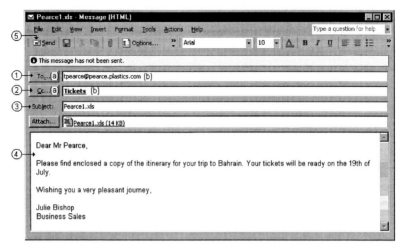

The e-mail application (Outlook 2002 in this example) opens a new mail message window. The attached file usually appears as an icon either in the lower part of the window or in the message header. Depending on the file format used (rich or plain text) the lower part of the window may be divided into one or two panes.

① Indicate the address(es) to which you want to send the message, separating names with a semicolon (b) or click (a) to select the names in an address book.

② If you want to send any copies, enter the addresses (b) or click (a) to select them from an address book.

③ If necessary, change the title of the message.

④ Click in this box then enter any comment or message you want to add.

⑤ Click to send your message and attached file.

⇨ To open or change an attachment, the recipient must open the message then double-click the attachment's icon. Opening this file will start the Excel application automatically.

⇨ To close the e-mail window without sending the message, click the ☒ button. If you made any changes to the message, Excel prompts you to save the document. If you click **Yes**, the document will be saved in the **Drafts** folder, or in the **Inbox** depending on your software. You can send it at a later time.

2.2 Managing worksheets

A-Creating a link between worksheets

This technique allows you to display in one sheet the contents of cells located on another sheet.

▓ Select the destination cells, type = and select the source cells.

▓ Validate.

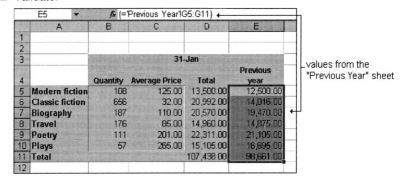

values from the "Previous Year" sheet

⇨ *You could also use the command **Edit - Paste Special - Paste Link**, after you have copied the source data using the **Edit - Copy command.***

B-Selecting sheets to create a workgroup

There are two main objectives when you select more than one sheet. Firstly you can group the sheets to make actions common to all of them (copying, deleting, etc.) and secondly, changes made to one of the sheets, such as entering or editing data or changes to the page setup, can be carried over to all the sheets in the workgroup.

▓ To select several adjacent worksheets, click the first sheet's tab, hold down the ⇧ Shift key and click the tab of the last sheet required.
To select several nonadjacent sheets, click the first sheet's tab, hold down the Ctrl key and click the tab of each other sheet you require.
To select all the sheets in the workbook, right-click one of the sheet tabs and choose the **Select All Sheets** option.

▓ To select a single sheet again, deactivating the workgroup, click the tab of a sheet that is not in the selected group or right-click the tab of one of the selected sheets and choose **Ungroup Sheets**.

When all the sheets in the workbook are selected, moving to another sheet will cancel the selection.

C-Copying/moving a sheet from one workbook to another

▧ Open the book from which you want to copy or move, and also the destination workbook.

▧ Activate the sheet you want to copy or move or select the sheets concerned.

▧ **Edit - Move or Copy Sheet**

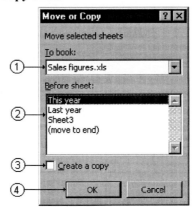

① Select the destination workbook.

② Select the existing sheet in front of which you want to insert.

③ Activate this option if you are making a copy.

④ Insert the sheet.

D-Moving one or more worksheets

▧ Select the tab(s) on the worksheet(s) you want to move.

▧ Drag the tab to move the sheet(s) to the new position.

E-Deleting/inserting worksheets

▧ Select the worksheet(s) to be deleted then use **Edit - Delete Sheet**.

▧ Click **Delete** to confirm.

⇨ *To insert a worksheet, select the worksheet (before which you want to insert a new sheet) then use Insert - Worksheet.*

F-Changing the colour of worksheet tabs

▧ Select the tab(s) concerned.

▧ Right-click the tab or one of the tabs if you have selected several.

▧ Choose the **Tab Color** option.

▧ Select the colour of your choice and click **OK** to confirm.

▒ Activate another tab to view the result.

⇨ *You can also use the **Format - Sheet - Tab Color** menu option to modify your selected tab(s).*

G-Naming a worksheet

▒ Double-click the tab of the sheet you are going to name then type the new name over the former one (you are limited to 31 characters). Press ⌷Enter⌷.

3.1 Entering data

A-Entering constants (text, values, dates, etc.)

▓ Activate the cell where you want the data to appear then type the data.

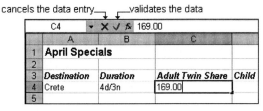

▓ Activate the next cell you want to fill in.

▷ *To enter several lines of data in a cell, press* ⌈Alt⌉ ⌈Enter⌉ *at the end of each line.*

▷ *To enter the same data in several cells, select all the cells concerned, type the data (a formula, perhaps) and press* ⌈Ctrl⌉⌈Enter⌉ *to enter.*

▷ *You can type in up to 32000 characters in each cell. If you enter £10000, Excel will apply the format £10, 000 immediately. To enter a percentage, type a % sign just after the number.*

▷ *If you deactivate the option* **Move Selection after Enter** *accessible via* **Tools - Options - Edit** *tab, this prevents* ⌈Enter⌉ *from activating the next cell.*

▷ *To indicate a negative value, precede the value with a minus sign (-) or enclose the value in brackets.*

▷ *By default, when you enter the last two figures of a date, Excel interprets them as follows:*

- from 00 to 29 = the year 2000 to 2029

- from 30 to 99 = 1930 to 1999.

▷ *If you use Windows 98, Windows 2000 or a later version, these parameters can be modified in the* **Date** *tab in the Windows* **Start** *menu, under* **Settings - Control Panel - Regional Settings.**

B-Inserting symbols

This technique inserts symbols that do not appear on your keyboard. A symbol can be inserted in an empty cell or within text while you are entering it.

▓ **Insert - Symbol - Symbols** tab

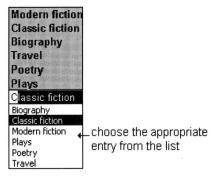

① Select the font that contains the character you want to insert.

② Select the required character.

③ Click to insert the character.

The Cancel button becomes a Close button.

▧ Close the dialog box with the **Close** button.

C-Entering data semi-automatically with AutoComplete

▧ Type in the first characters: Excel proposes an existing entry which begins with the same characters. To accept, press Enter .

▧ You can also see the list of existing entries in the column by pressing Alt ↓ .

Modern fiction
Classic fiction
Biography
Travel
Poetry
Plays

Classic fiction
Biography
Classic fiction
Modern fiction
Plays
Poetry
Travel

← choose the appropriate entry from the list

⇨ *The option **Pick from List** in the shortcut menu displays the same list.*

⇨ *This function operates only if the **Enable AutoComplete for cell values** option is active in the **Options** dialog box (**Tools - Options - Edit** tab).*

D-Inserting the control date into a cell

▦ Activate the cell where you want to display the date.
▦ There are three ways to insert the computer's control date:

=TODAY()	The control date, updated each time the sheet is opened.
=NOW()	The control date and time, updated when the sheet is opened.
[Ctrl] ;	The control date, not changed automatically.

▦ Enter.

E-Entering the same data in several cells

▦ Select the range of cells concerned.
▦ Enter the formula or text common to all these cells.

If you are entering a formula, enter it as it should appear in the active cell of the selected range.

▦ Validate with [Ctrl][Enter].

F-Entering several lines of text in the same cell

▦ Activate the cell where you want to type the text, then enter the text, pressing [Alt][Enter] when you want to change line.
▦ Enter to confirm your cell contents.

G-Creating a series of data

Creating a simple series

La data series is a logical progression

▦ Enter the first value in the series.
▦ Drag the fill handle from the bottom right of that cell to the last target cell for the series.

▓ When you reach the end of your series, the **Auto Fill Options** button  appears to the bottom right of the series. If you click this button, you can (depending on the type of series, and your needs) choose an option to modify the way the values are copied or incremented.

Creating a complex series

▓ Enter the first value in the series then select the cell containing that value.

▓ **Edit - Fill - Series**

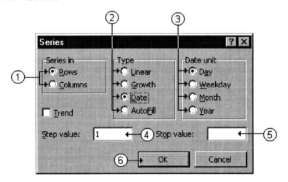

① Indicate whether the series should be inserted in **Rows** or **Columns**.

② Specify the type of series you are making.

③ If you choose a **Date** type, give the **Date unit** in the right hand frame.

④ Modify the increment value as necessary.

⑤ Indicate the last value in the series.

⑥ Click to confirm.

⇨ *You can also select the first two values in the series to indicate the interval you want to use. For example, **Jan** and **Mar** were selected to create the following series:*

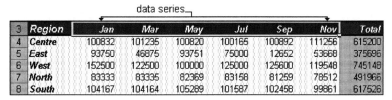

data series

Region	Jan	Mar	May	Jul	Sep	Nov	Total
Centre	100832	101235	100820	100165	100892	111256	615200
East	93750	46875	93751	75000	12652	53668	375696
West	152500	122500	100000	125000	125600	119548	745148
North	83333	83335	82369	83158	81259	78512	491966
South	104167	104164	105289	101587	102458	99861	617526

H-Creating a custom data series

▓ Tools - Options - Custom Lists tab

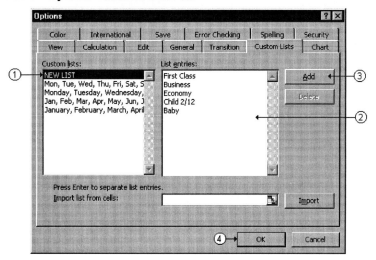

① Click **NEW LIST**.
② Enter the data, pressing `Enter` to separate each entry.
③ Create the list.
④ Click to confirm and close the dialog box.

⇨ *The first character of an entry cannot be a number.*

I- Attaching comments to cells

Creating a comment

▓ Activate the cell where you want to make a comment then use the **Insert - Comment** menu option or `⇧ Shift` `F2`.

▓ Enter the text in the comment box.

The comment is entered directly into a ScreenTip. Use `Enter` to change lines.

▓ Press ⌜Esc⌝ or click outside the box.

*A red triangle marks the top right corner of a cell that contains a comment. This indicator is visible only when one of the comment indicator options is active in the **Options** dialog box (**Tools** - **Options** - **View** tab).*

Displaying a comment

▓ Point to the cell that contains the red triangle.

▓ If the triangle is not visible, use the buttons from the **Reviewing** bar:

  To scroll through the comments concerning the current worksheet.

  To show/hide all the comments.

▷ *To edit a comment, select the corresponding cell, then click* 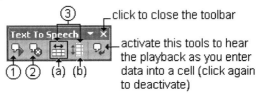 *on the **Reviewing** toolbar. To delete a comment, select the cell concerned, then click* .

J- Using speech playback

▓ Show the **Text To Speech** toolbar with **View - Toolbars - Text To Speech**.

▓ To hear the contents of cells that have already been entered on the worksheet, select those cells.

③

click to close the toolbar

activate this tools to hear the playback as you enter data into a cell (click again to deactivate)

① ② (a) (b)

① Click this tool button to hear Excel read what is displayed in the selected cells.

② To pause the playback, click this tool button. To resume the playback, clic again.

③ To change the order in which Excel reads cell ranges, click (a) for Excel to read all the cells to the right of the active cell then those on the next row or (b) to read down from the active cell then from the next column on the right and so on.

▷ *You can choose a different voice and reading speed for you computer, in the Windows **Control Panel**, double-click the **Speech** folder and under the **Text To Speech** tab, choose a voice from the **Voice selection** list; if required, use the **Voice speed** cursor to speed up or slow down the voice.*

3.2 Editing data

A-Modifying cell contents

▓ Double-click the cell concerned.

▓ Make the changes (the ⌊Ins⌋ key switches between Insert mode and Over-
type mode) then enter.

⇨ *You can also click the cell then edit its contents in the formula bar.*

B-Clearing cell contents

▓ Select the cells to be cleared.

▓ Drag the fill handle backwards over the selected cells to clear their contents.

⇨ *This technique deletes the contents of the cells without affecting their*
*format. The command **Edit - Clear** allows you to indicate exactly what*
*should be cleared (**Formats, Contents, Comments**, etc.).*

C-Replacing cell contents and/or formats

Replacing text

▓ If the replacement is to be carried out over the active worksheet or all the
worksheets in the workbook, activate a single cell. To make the replacement in a portion of the active sheet, select the range of cells concerned.

▓ **Edit - Replace** or ⌊Ctrl⌋ **H**

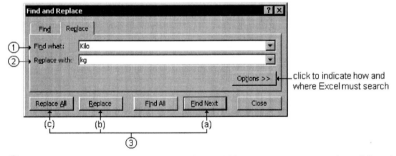

① Enter the text you wish to replace (this zone can contain wildcard
characters: ? is a substitute for one character; * is a substitute for
several).

② Enter the replacement text.

③ The replacements can be made individually (buttons (a) and (b)), or all
at once (button (c)).

Replacing formatting

▧ Activate a cell or select the specific range of cells involved.

▧ **Edit - Replace** or [Ctrl] **H**

▧ If necessary, click the **Options** button to show all the search options.

▧ Delete any text that may be in the **Find what** or **Replace with** boxes.

▧ Click the first **Format** button and in the **Find Format** dialog box, select the required format options.

*The **Choose Format From Cell** button is used to select a cell and retrieve that cell's formatting automatically.*

▧ Click **OK**, in the **Find Format** dialog box.

▧ Click the second **Format** button and in the **Find Format** dialog box, select the required format options and click **OK**.

▧ Make your replacements one by one using the **Find Next** and **Replace** buttons or use the **Replace All** button to make all the replacements with one action.

▧ Click the **Close** button.

⇨ *You can replace text and formatting simultaneously. If you want to do this, enter the text in the **Find what** or **Replace with** boxes and choose the format options by clicking the **Format** buttons.*

D-Sorting data in a table

▧ Select the table you want to sort.

▧ To sort by one criterion, activate a cell in the column you want to sort by.

▧ Then use to sort in ascending order or to sort in descending order.

⇨ *To sort by several criteria, use the **Data - Sort** command.*

E-Checking the spelling in a text

▧ To check the whole worksheet, activate any cell. To check part of the text, select it.

▧ **Tools**   [ABC✓]   [F7]
Spelling

Excel reads the text, stopping at each unrecognised word. A word may be unrecognised, because it is absent from Excel's dictionary, because it contains an unusual combination of lower case and capital letters, or because it is typed twice.

Spelling is checked against Excel's main dictionary, and against as many personal dictionaries as you wish (by default, the only existing one is CUSTOM.DIC).

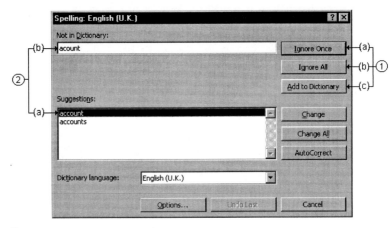

① If the word is correctly spelt, click:

    (a)   to leave the word unchanged and continue the check.

    (b)   to leave a particular word unchanged each time it occurs in the text.

    (c)   to add the word to the current dictionary.

③ If the word contains a mistake, correct it by a double-click on one of the suggestions (a) or enter the correct spelling (b).

Next, click **Change** to replace the incorrect word with the correct one, or **Change All** to replace the incorrect word with the correct one each time it occurs.

▨ For a word which is repeated by mistake, click **Delete** to remove the repeated word.

▨ At the end of the spelling check, a dialog box appears:

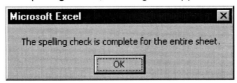

▨ Click **OK**.

3.3 Copying and moving data

A-Copying data into adjacent cells

▦ Activate the cell you want to copy then point to its fill handle.

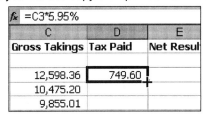

▦ Drag the fill handle to the last destination cell for the copy then release the mouse button.

▦ Specify how you want to copy, by clicking the **Auto Fill Options** button ⊞ at the bottom right of the copied range:

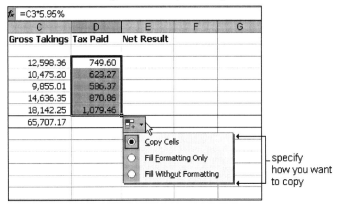

B-Copying and moving cells

▦ Select the source cells.

▦ Point to the edge of the selected range.

		1st Quarter	2nd Quarter
4	WESTERN	1,250.00	1,210.00
5	SOUTHERN	1,000.00	990.00
6	NORTHERN	1,500.00	1,420.00
7	EASTERN	1,125.00	1,120.00
8	Average	1,218.75	1,185.00
9	Total	4,875.00	4,740.00

- If you are copying, press the ⌈Ctrl⌉ key and, without releasing it, drag the cells to their destination.

  If the cells are being moved, just drag the cells to their new position.
- Release first the mouse button, then the ⌈Ctrl⌉ key, if you have been using it.

⇨ *To move a range of cells to another worksheet, hold down the ⌈Alt⌉ key as you drag the selected range onto the tab of the sheet concerned then to the first cell of the destination range. To copy cells to another worksheet, hold down both the ⌈Ctrl⌉ and ⌈Alt⌉ keys as you drag.*

- Select the source cells.
- If you are copying the cells, use:

Edit		
Copy	📋	⌈Ctrl⌉ **C**

- If you are moving the cells, use:

Edit		
Cut	✂	⌈Ctrl⌉ **X**

- Activate the first cell of the destination range.

Edit		
Paste	📋	⌈Ctrl⌉ **V**

*When you paste copied data, the **Paste** button 📋 appears to the bottom right of the destination range, providing further options relating to what can be pasted.*

⇨ *If the Clipboard task pane is visible, you can click the icon of the item you want to paste.*

C-Transposing rows and columns while copying

- Select the data to be copied, use **Edit - Copy** then activate the first destination cell.
- **Edit - Paste Special**

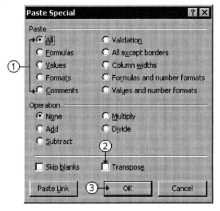

① Activate the option corresponding to what you are copying.

② Activate this option.

③ Click **OK**.

⇨ *Another technique you could use is to activate the destination cell, expand the list on the* *tool button and choose the **Transpose** option.*

D-Copying cells into several sheets

▨ Select the cells you want to copy.

▨ Select the other worksheets involved, by holding down Ctrl and clicking their tabs.

▨ **Edit - Fill - Across Worksheets**

▨ As required, choose to copy **All** or just the **Formats** or just the **Contents**.

▨ Click **OK**.

⇨ *You can also use the drag and drop method to copy cells to another sheet. Select the cells then hold down* Ctrl *and* Alt*; drag the cells to the tab of the required sheet then to the destination cells on that sheet.*

E-Copying/moving multiple items

*If the **Show Office Clipboard Automatically** option is active (find this by clicking the **Options** button at the bottom of the **Clipboard** task pane), the **Clipboard** task pane appears automatically as soon as you have made two consecutive move or copy actions or once you have used* Ctrl *C twice.*

▨ Select the cells concerned and transfer them into the clipboard using **Cut** or **Copy**. This can be done as many times as necessary.

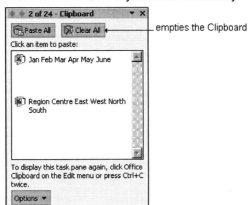

The *Office Clipboard* contains all the items (a maximum of 24) cut or copied from the various Office applications (Excel, Word, PowerPoint etc.).

- To paste one of the items from the **Clipboard** task pane, activate the first destination cell then click that item.
- Insert each item from the **Clipboard** task pane in this way, as many times as required.

  *When you point to an item, an arrow appears on its right. Click this arrow to see options allowing you to **Paste** or **Delete** the item.*

- If necessary, close the **Clipboard** task pane by clicking its ☒ button.

⇨ *The ▣ Paste All button on the **Clipboard** task pane pastes all the items within. They are pasted in a column, from top to bottom. This button is unavailable when there is a picture or object in the list.*

F- Reproducing a format

- Select the cells whose formats you want to copy then click ✎ on the **Standard** toolbar.

  A paintbrush appears under the mouse pointer.

- Select the cells to which you want to apply the format.

⇨ *You can also copy formats by making a standard copy/paste operation then clicking the **Paste** button ▣ at the bottom of the copied cells and choosing the **Formatting only** option. The original cell values are not altered.*

⇨ *If the formatting has to be reproduced several times, double-click the ✎ tool button. Press ⎋ to cancel this function.*

G-Copying formats, displayed values or cell contents, with or without a link

- Select the cells containing the results or formats you want to copy.
- Go into **Edit - Copy**.
- Activate the first cell of the destination cell range.
- Open the list attached to the ▣ ▾ tool button:

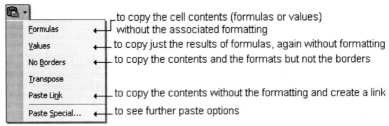

to copy the cell contents (formulas or values) without the associated formatting
to copy just the results of formulas, again without formatting
to copy the contents and the formats but not the borders
to copy the contents without the formatting and create a link
to see further paste options

⇨ *These options can also be found using the **Edit - Paste Special** command.*

H-Making simple calculations while you copy

▓ Select the data you wish to copy and start the copying process (**Edit - Copy**).

▓ Activate the first destination cell (the target cells must contain some data).

▓ **Edit - Paste Special**

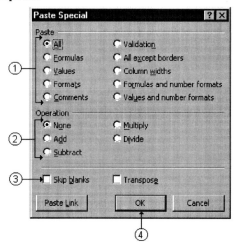

① Choose which elements you wish to copy.

② Specify the operation you wish to perform.

③ If you want to omit any empty cells in the selection, tick this check box.

④ Click to confirm.

I- Copying Excel data into another application and establishing a link

When a link is in place, any changes made to the data in the original Excel workbook are carried over into the file containing the exported data.

▓ Open the Excel workbook containing the data you want to copy.

▓ **Edit**   Ctrl C
  Copy

▓ Open the other application and the document into which you want to paste the Excel data.

▓ Put the insertion point where the data should be pasted.

▓ **Edit - Paste Special**

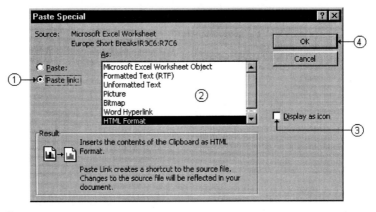

① Activate this option.

② Select the format in which you want to paste the data.

③ Activate this option if you want the linked data to be displayed in the form of an icon.

④ Click to confirm.

3.4 Named ranges

A- Naming cell ranges

First method

Select the range of cells which you want to name then use the command **Insert** - **Name** - **Define** or Ctrl F3 .

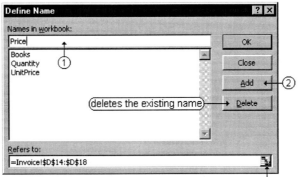

click to collapse the dialog box so you can select items, or modify a selection, on the worksheet

① Enter the name for the range.

② Add the new name to the list.

▦ Go on to define any other names then click **OK**.

⇨ *There must be no spaces or hyphens in these names.*

⇨ *To name a calculation formula, enter the formula in the **Refers to** box. To use a formula with a name, type = followed by the name of the formula, and enter.*

Second method

This method is useful if the names that you want to apply to the cells are adjacent to them.

▦ Select the cells containing the names to be used and the cells that you want to name.

▦ **Insert** - **Name** - **Create** or [Ctrl] [⇧ Shift] [F3]

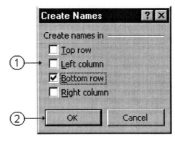

① Indicate the position of the cells containing the names.

② Click to confirm.

B-Modifying named ranges

Changing which cells are associated with the name

▦ Select the new range of cells required then use **Insert** - **Name** - **Define** or [Ctrl] [F3].

▦ Enter the new name.

You must type in the name again and not simply select it from the list of names.

▦ Click the **Add** button.

⇨ *You can also redefine the cells in a named range by selecting the range name in the **Define Name** dialog box, clicking the* ▦ *button and selecting the new cells in the worksheet.*

Changing the name of the range

▓ **Insert - Name - Define** or `Ctrl` `F3`

▓ In the list, select the name concerned.

▓ Enter the new name in the **Names in workbook** box then click the **Add** button.

This action does not delete the previous name; if you wish, delete that from the list.

▓ Click **OK.**

C-Selecting a range of cells by its name

▓ Click the ▼ button on the left of the formula bar.

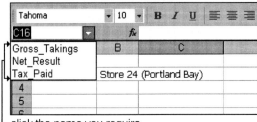

└click the name you require

D-Displaying a list of names and associated references

▓ Activate the cell from which the list of names should appear.

▓ **Insert - Name - Paste**

▓ Click the **Paste List** button.

4.1 Calculations

A-Entering a calculation formula

▓ Activate the cell which will display the result.

▓ Type =

▓ Activate the first cell involved in the calculation (click the cell or use the arrow keys to move the pointer).

▓ Indicate the mathematical operation to perform.

▓ Repeat for each of the cells involved in the calculation:

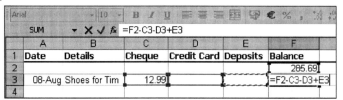

▓ When you reach the last cell, either click the ☑ button on the formula bar or press the ⌜Enter⌟ key.

⇨ *If you know the cell references you can type them in rather than using the mouse or arrow keys to point to them.*

B-Calculating with values from more than one sheet

You can enter a formula into one worksheet that refers to cells on a different worksheet.

▓ Activate the cell that is going to display the result.

▓ Type =

▓ Start the formula and at the appropriate place, click the tab of the required sheet, select the cell(s) you require, enter the required arithmetic operator and finish the formula.

▓ Press ⌜Enter⌟ to confirm.

	B5	▾	*fx* =This year'!F4-'Last year'!F4		
	A	B	C	D	E
3					
4		Books	Music	IT	Other
5	WEST	150			
6	SOUTH				
7	NORTH				
8	EAST				
9	Average				
10					

Cell B5 subtracts the value of cell F4 of the "Last Year" sheet from the value of cell F4 of the "This Year" sheet.

⇨ *You can also calculate values from several different workbooks. When doing this, make sure all the workbooks are open. Use the **Window** menu to go to a cell in a worksheet in a different workbook.*

C-Adding up a group of cells

▦ Activate the cell which is going to display the result.

▦ Click 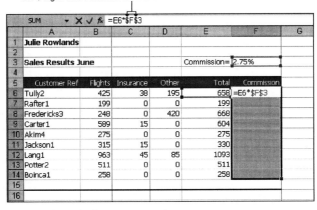.

	A	B	C
	SUM ▾ ✗ ✓ ƒ×	=SUM(B23:B26)	
20			
21	Payment details		
22			
23	Flight Only	316.00	
24	Insurance	16.00	
25	Airport Taxes	18.00	
26	Visa/ETA	6.50	
27	TOTAL AMOUNT DUE	=SUM(B23:B26)	
28		SUM(number1, [number2], ...)	
29			
30	Payment Due	30 June 2001	
31			

▦ If you are not satisfied with this selection, change it.

▦ Press Enter or click the ✓ button.

D-Including an absolute cell reference in a formula

An absolute cell reference does not evolve when the formula is copied.

▦ Start entering the formula, stopping after the cell reference that you want to make absolute. If you are editing an existing formula, position the insertion point after the cell reference.

▦ Press F4.

the $ signs show that the row and column references are absolute

	A	B	C	D	E	F	G
	SUM ▾ ✗ ✓ ƒ×	=E6*$F$3					
1	Julie Rowlands						
2							
3	Sales Results June				Commission=	2.75%	
4							
5	Customer Ref	Flights	Insurance	Other	Total	Commission	
6	Tully2	425	38	195	658	=E6*$F$3	
7	Rafter1	199	0	0	199		
8	Fredericks3	248	0	420	668		
9	Carter1	589	15	0	604		
10	Akim4	275	0	0	275		
11	Jackson1	315	15	0	330		
12	Lang1	963	45	85	1093		
13	Potter2	511	0	0	511		
14	Boinca1	258	0	0	258		
15							
16							

▦ Complete the formula if necessary, then enter.

Microsoft Excel 2002

CALCULATION

⇨ *Press* F4 *again for only the row number to remain absolute, and again for the column number.*

E- Using simple statistical functions

▓ Click the cell where the result will be displayed then open the list on the ∑ ▾ tool button by clicking the black arrow.

▓ Click the required function:

Average to calculate the average of a set of cells.

Count to count up within a set of cells the number of cells containing numerical values.

Max to extract the highest value from a group of cells.

Min to extract the lowest value from a group of cells.

▓ If the suggested selection is incorrect, modify it.

▓ Confirm.

F- Inserting a function

▓ Click the cell where the result will be displayed.

▓ Click the *fx* button on the formula bar or use the **Insert - Function** command.

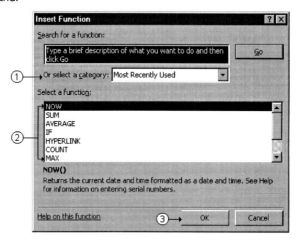

① If necessary, change the category.

② Choose your required function from the list.

③ Click to confirm.

▓ To set each argument within the function:

  – click the corresponding text box and click the ▨ button,

  – on the worksheet, select the cell(s) corresponding to the argument,

  – click ▨ to restore the dialog box.

▓ When you have defined all the arguments, click **OK**.

⇨ *You can also insert a function within a formula or within another function. To do this, start the formula and at the appropriate place click the*  *button on the formula bar. This displays a list of the last functions used and the* **More Functions** *option which takes you to a full list of functions.*

⇨ *To find a function easily, enter a brief description of the result you wish to obtain in the* **Search for a function** *text box on the* **Insert Function** *dialog box (Insert - Function) and click* **OK** *at the top of the dialog box. Excel will display a list of functions corresponding to your request.*

⇨ *If you know the formula you want to use, you can enter it directly into the cell. If you do this, a ScreenTip appears, showing the different arguments you must set.*

G-Using named ranges in calculations

Using a name in a formula

▓ Start entering the formula then stop where the name is required.

▓ **Insert - Name - Paste** or [F3]

double-click the name
of the range you want

Paste Name

Paste name

Commerce
Finance
Marketing

OK   Cancel

▓ Complete the formula.

⇨ *You can also enter the name directly into the formula, instead of indicating the cell references.*

Replacing cell references with their names

▓ Select the cells containing the formulas you want to modify.

▓ **Insert - Name - Apply**

▓ Click all the names concerned. If you select a name by mistake, click it again to deselect it.

▓ Click **OK**.

If you select names that are inappropriate for that formula, Excel ignores those names.

H-Setting a condition in a formula

▓ Activate the cell where you want to display the result.

▓ Enter your condition, taking care to follow the syntax:
=IF(condition,action if TRUE,action if FALSE)

You can insert the IF function and set each argument in the **Function**
Arguments *dialog box or enter the formula directly into the cell.*

	C3 ▼	*fx* =IF(B3>=58,"Pass","")		
	A	**B**	**C**	
1				
2	Student Name	Final Marks	Subject Result	
3	BAILEY Claire	69	Pass	
4	EVANS David	52		
5	JAKOVIC Elena	88	Pass	
6	MCPHERSON Anne	73	Pass	
7	NASH Elizabeth	54		
8	TAYLOR Duncan	68	Pass	
9				

*If the student's mark in cell B3 equals or is higher than 58, the text
"Pass" is displayed in the cell; if the mark is lower, no text is displayed.*

⇨ *A variety of actions can be performed in a conditional expression:*

Display a number	enter the number,
Display a text	enter the text between quotation marks,
Display the result	enter the calculation formula,
of a calculation	
Display the contents	enter to the cell,
of a cell	
No display	type "".

⇨ *For conditions, several operators are available:*

>	greater than
<	less than
<>	different from
>=	greater than or equal to
<=	less than or equal to.

⇨ *You can set multiple conditions, linking them with the operators AND
and/or OR:*
**=IF(AND(cond1,cond2, ...,condn),action to be carried out if all the
conditions are satisfied,action to be carried out if any condition is
not satisfied)**
**=IF(OR(cond1,cond2, ...,condn),action to be carried out if at least
one condition is satisfied, action to be carried out if no condition is
satisfied)**

I- Calculating with dates and using date functions

▨ If you are calculating in days, proceed as for other calculations, since any date entered is treated as a number of days.

▨ To add a number of months to a start date, use the following syntax:
=DATE(YEAR(start_date),MONTH(start_date)+
period_in_months, DAY(start_date))

▨ To add a number of years, use:
=DATE(YEAR(start_date)+period_in_years,
MONTH(start_date),DAY(start_date))
For example to calculate the date two months from now, use:
=DATE(YEAR(NOW()),MONTH(NOW())+2,DAY(NOW()))

⇨ *If the results of your calculations are four years ahead of what they ought to be, deactivate the **1904 date system** option in **Tools - Options - Calculation** tab.*

J- Using lookup functions

The structure of the source table

▨ A table is made up of a column (or row) containing the compare values and other columns (rows) listing information associated with these values.

▨ The column (row) containing the compare values should be in the first position.

Using the VLOOKUP and HLOOKUP function

As a rule, data in a table are organised in columns, which is why you generally use the VLOOKUP (V for vertical) function. If the data are organised in rows, you would use the HLOOKUP function (H for horizontal).

▨ Sort the table in ascending order on the data in the first column.

▨ In the cell where you want to display certain information from the table, use the following function:
VLOOKUP (lookup_value,table_array,col_index_num,range_lookup)

Lookup_value	refers to the compare value, a value that can be entered into the cell or directly in the formula.
Table_array	is the table of values.
Col_index_num	is the number of the column containing the value you are seeking (numbering begins at the first column in the table).
Range_lookup	if entered as FALSE, this looks for an exact match or returns an error.

	K3	▼	f_x =IF(J3="","",VLOOKUP(J3,booklist,2,FALSE))		

	J	K	L	M	N
1					
2	ISBN	Title	Price	Quantity	Total
3	0012458758	Persuasion			
4	0152622842	Wuthering Heights			
5	0014252052	Wild Swans			
6					
7					

The function shown above looks in the second column of the "booklist" range to find the title that corresponds to the ISBN entered.

K-Making Euro currency conversions

▓ **Tools - Euro Conversion**

*If the **Euro Conversion** command is unavailable, you should install the corresponding add-in, by choosing **Tools - Add-Ins** and activating the **Euro Currency Tools** option in the **Add-Ins available** list. If this add-in does not appear in the list, click the **Browse** button to look for it and install it. If you see a message informing you that the necessary component is not installed, click **Yes** to confirm the installation (you may need to insert the Excel 2002 or Office XP CD-ROM).*

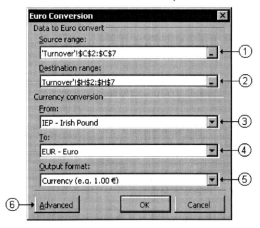

① Click this button to select the cell or (consecutive) cells containing the values you wish to convert and click ▣ to restore the dialog box.

② Click this button then select the cell in which you wish to paste the converted values and click ▣.

③ Choose the currency from which you are converting.

④ Choose the target currency for the conversion.

⑤ Select the format you want the converted values to use:

Currency   to apply a currency format corresponding to the currency chosen in the **To** list and reproduce the format of the source cells (borders, font, etc.).

ISO   to display the corresponding ISO code for the currency chosen in the **To** list and reproduce the format of the source cells.

(none)   to keep the current number format and formatting of the target cells.

⑥ If the source range contains formulas or you wish to verify the rounding system, click this button.

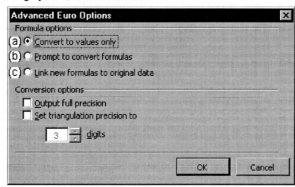

From the **Formula options**, choose exactly what you want to do:

(a)   Excel shows the result of any formulas converted into euros (default option)

(b)   for each formula, Excel will offer you several options before converting.

(c)   Excel uses the EuroConvert function, linking the result to the source data.

If you do not want to use the European Union's currency rounding rules and control the rounding system yourself, choose from the options in the **Conversion options** frame:

  – tick the **Output full precision** option for Excel to include all the significant figures in the converted values without rounding.

  – tick the **Set triangulation precision to** option and indicate the number of **digits** to use when calculating the rounding. This option may be useful if you are converting two Euro zone currencies (from Irish pounds to French francs, for example), with the calculation being based on an intermediate conversion into euros.

Click **OK** once, then click **OK** again.

If you asked Excel to **Prompt to convert formulas** in the **Advanced Euro Options** dialog box, this dialog box will appear whenever Excel tries to convert a cell containing a formula:

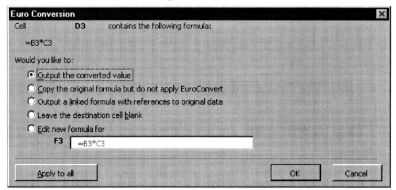

In this case, choose how the conversion should be carried out then click **OK** to go onto the next formula or click **Apply to all** to use these settings for all formulas.

L- Finding a function

Help - Microsoft Excel Help or F1

If the Office Assistant appears, click its **Options** button, deactivate the **Use the Office Assistant** check box, click **OK** then use **Help - Microsoft Excel Help** again.

Activate the **Contents** tab.

Expand the **Microsoft Excel Help** category, if necessary, by clicking the ⊞ sign, expand the **Function Reference** category by clicking ⊞.

Expand one of the categories of functions.

When you select a function in the left pane of the window, the syntax and a description of the function appears in the right pane.

4.2 Complex calculations

A-Adding statistics to a table

By inserting automatic subtotals, you can obtain rows of statistics. This is an easy way to summarise the information in a table.

▓ Sort the table by the column containing the entries you want to group together, as a first step to producing a subtotal for each group.

▓ Select the table then choose **Data - Subtotals**.

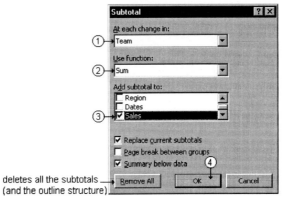

① Select the column used for grouping.

② Choose the type of statistic you require.

③ Mark the columns containing the values involved in the calculation.

④ Click to confirm.

1 2 3		A	B	C	D
	1	Team	Region	Dates	Sales
	2	Cierzniak	West	10-Jan	99.86
	3	Cierzniak	West	17-Jan	93.76
	4	Cierzniak	Centre	24-Jan	50.00
	5	Cierzniak	West	24-Jan	50.00
	6	Cierzniak	East	31-Jan	18.75
	7	Cierzniak	West	31-Jan	104.16
	8	Cierzniak	West	07-Feb	100.00
	9	Cierzniak	Centre	07-Feb	35.29
	10	Cierzniak	West	14-Feb	108.33
	11	**Cierzniak Total**			660.15
	12	Dillon	North	10-Jan	152.50
	13	Dillon	North	17-Jan	122.53
	14	Dillon	North	24-Jan	100.00
	15	Dillon	East	24-Jan	46.87
	16	Dillon	East	31-Jan	18.75
	17	Dillon	North	31-Jan	125.00
	18	Dillon	North	07-Feb	125.00
	19	Dillon	North	14-Feb	100.00
	20	Dillon	Centre	14-Feb	33.83
	21	**Dillon Total**			824.48
	22	Hardy	East	10-Jan	93.75

Excel calculates the statistics required and constructs an outline.

B-Consolidating worksheets

*This technique enables you to carry out an analysis (for example, a sum)
of values contained in several tables.*

▓ Activate the first cell of the range where you want to display the results.

▓ **Data - Consolidate**

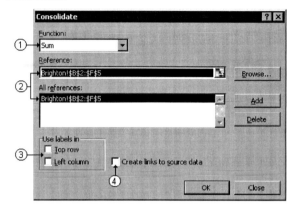

① Choose the calculation you want to perform.

② For each sheet to be consolidated: activate it and select the cells concerned then click the **Add** button.

③ If you have included data labels in your selection, indicate where they
are located.

④ If you wish to create a permanent link between the source sheets and
the destination sheet, activate this check box.

C-Creating a two-input table

	A6 ▼	ƒₓ =ABS(PMT(B2/12,B3,B1))				
	A	B	C	D	E	F
1	Capital	5,000.00				
2	Interest rate	11%				
3	Instalments	12				
4			(number of instalments)			
5						
6	441.91	12	18	24	30	36
7	5,000.00	441.91	302.59	233.04	191.39	163.69
8	10,000.00	883.82	605.19	466.08	382.78	327.39
9	15,000.00	1,325.72	907.78	699.12	574.17	491.08
10	20,000.00	1,767.63	1,210.37	932.16	765.56	654.77
11	25,000.00	2,209.54	1,512.96	1,165.20	956.95	818.47
12	30,000.00	2,651.45	1,815.56	1,398.24	1,148.34	982.16
13	35,000.00	3,093.36	2,118.15	1,631.27	1,339.73	1,145.86
14	40,000.00	3,535.27	2,420.74	1,864.31	1,531.12	1,309.55
15	45,000.00	3,977.17	2,723.33	2,097.35	1,722.51	1,473.24
16	50,000.00	4,419.08	3,025.93	2,330.39	1,913.90	1,636.94

this cell contains
the calculation
formula

amount borrowed   results of the calculation

*The table below shows how the amount paid back monthly on a loan
varies according to the number of instalments and the sum borrowed.*

- In cells located outside the table, enter the initial input values for the calculation.
- Enter the variable data, one series in a row, and the other series in a column.
- At the intersection of the row and the column enter the calculation formula, referring to the input cells outside the table.
- Select the range of cells including the formula and all the result cells.
- **Data - Table**
- In the **Row input cell** box, indicate which input cell corresponds to the variable data in the row.
- In the **Column input cell** box, indicate which input cell formula corresponds to the column data.
- Click **OK** to confirm.

⇨ *Excel does not recalculate the table automatically.*

D-Calculating with array formulas

- To create an array formula, proceed as for an ordinary calculation, but instead of working on individual cells, work on a selected range of cells and enter using [Ctrl][⇧ Shift][Enter], instead of [Enter] or [Ctrl][Enter].

B12	▼	ƒx {=(B4:D7-E4:E7)/E4:E7}			
	A	B	C	D	E	F

Number of employees by job category and by country for all subsidiaries

	CANADA	GREAT BRITAIN	IRELAND	Average
Accountant	50	55	44	50
Secretary	220	275	225	240
Warehouse Foreman	15	20	12	16
Lorry Driver	160	175	125	153

% difference with respect to Group average

	CANADA	GREAT BRITAIN	IRELAND
Accountant	0.67%	10.74%	-11.41%
Secretary	-8.33%	14.58%	-6.25%
Warehouse Foreman	-4.26%	27.66%	-23.40%
Lorry Driver	4.35%	14.13%	-18.48%

You can recognise an array formula by the braces surrounding it.

⇨ *Some functions can be applied only using array formulas. An array formula also takes up less memory space than a group of ordinary formulas.*

E-Setting a goal value

▒ Activate the cell you wish to set to a certain value and ensure that it contains a calculation formula.

▒ **Tools - Goal Seek**

▒ Set the goal value in the **To value** box and indicate the variable cell in **By changing cell**.

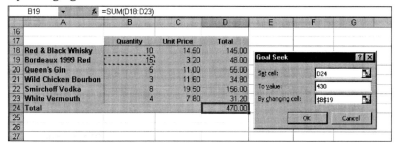

The spending budget is 430. The buyer has decided to economise on wine. How many bottles can he still purchase?

▒ Click **OK**.

As soon as Excel finds a solution, it displays its results on the worksheet.

▒ To accept the result suggested by Excel, click **OK**. The new values are incorporated into the sheet. To return to the original values, click **Cancel**.

F-Making scenarios

A scenario enables you to solve a problem by considering several hypotheses.

Creating scenarios

▒ **Tools - Scenarios**

▒ Click the **Add** button.

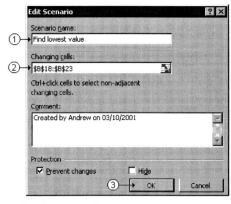

① Enter a name for the scenario.

② Delete whatever appears in the **Changing cells** box, click  and hold down Ctrl while selecting from the sheet the cells with the values to vary in this scenario. Next, click 🔽.

③ Click **OK** then enter the values for each changing cell and click **OK** again.

Using a scenario

▓ **Tools - Scenarios**

▓ If you want to run only one scenario, select it then click **Show** (the result replaces the current values on your worksheet). If you want a summary report of all the scenarios, click **Summary**.

▓ If necessary, select the cells whose results interest you.

▓ Click **OK**.

The summary is presented as an outline on a separate worksheet.

4.3 Auditing

A-Showing/hiding the Formula Auditing toolbar

▓ **Tools - Formula Auditing - Show Formula Auditing Toolbar**

B-Displaying formulas instead of results

▓ **Tools - Formula Auditing - Formula Auditing Mode** or Ctrl '

▓ Use the same command or shortcut key to display results once again.

C-Analysing errors in formulas

▦ In the **Options** dialog box (**Tools - Options - Error Checking** tab), check that the **Enable background error checking** option is active and if necessary, change the type of errors that Excel should find by activating or deactivating the various **Rules**.

Analysing errors in one formula

▦ Activate the cell containing the error, indicated by a coloured triangle (green by default) in the upper left corner of the cell.

▦ Click the ⟨!⟩ button.

A list of options appears (the first option reminds you what type of error has been made).

14					
15		CANADA	GREAT BRITAIN	IRELAND	AVERAGE
16	Accountant			⟨!⟩ ▾	#VALUE!
17	Secretary				Error in Value
18	Warehouse Foreman				Help on this error (a)
19	Lorry Driver				Show Calculation Steps... (b)
20					
21					Ignore Error (c)
22					
23					Edit in Formula Bar (d)
24					Error Checking Options... (e)
25					Show Formula Auditing Toolbar (f)
26					
27					

Click the option of your choice:

(a)   Displays the help window.

(b)   Shows the **Evaluate Formula** dialog box (cf. the next section).

(c)   Deactivates the error indicator: both the coloured triangle and the tag disappear.

(d)   Places the insertion point in the formula bar so you can modify the formula.

(e)   Shows the **Options** dialog box so you can choose which **Rules** Excel uses for **Error Checking**.

(f)   Displays the **Formula Auditing** toolbar.

Depending on the type of error, other options may appear.

Analysing errors in all the formulas

▦ Activate the worksheet you wish to check for errors.

▦ **Tools**
  Error Checking   ⟨◇⟩ on the **Formula Auditing** toolbar

Excel selects the first cell containing a mistake and in the **Error Checking** *dialog box, shows the formula and the error in detail.*

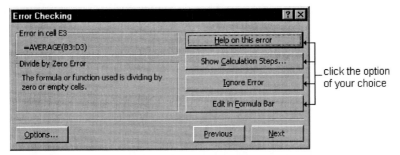

The buttons on the **Error Checking** dialog box may differ depending on the type of error.

▒ Depending on the option you choose, the **Restart** button may appear in the **Error Checking** dialog box which enables you to continue checking the worksheet.

▒ If you wish to go on to the next or previous error without working on the current one, click the **Next** or **Previous** button.

⇨ *The Reset Ignored Errors button (Tools - Options - Error Checking tab) reactivates error indicators in cells where you have chosen the Ignore Error option.*

Finding the cells that are causing an error

When a formula result shows an error value in a cell, such as #NAME?, #N/A or #DIV/0!, you can trace all the cells that are involved in that formula.

▒ Activate the cell containing the error.

▒ Click ⟨image⟩ on the **Formula Auditing** toolbar.

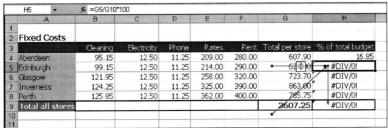

Auditing arrows appear on the screen. Red arrows link the cell that produced the error to those to which it refers, while the blue arrows show the precedents of the cell that caused the error initially.

⇨ *To clear the auditing arrows, click the ⟨image⟩ tool button on the Formula Auditing toolbar.*

D-Evaluating formulas

This technique can be used to see the result of each part of a nested formula.

▓ Select the cell you wish to evaluate.

▓ **Tools**
Formula Auditing on the **Formula Auditing** toolbar
Evaluate Formula

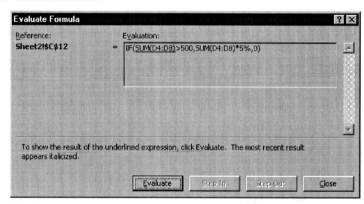

▓ Click **Evaluate** to see the result of the expression underlined in the **Evaluation** box. The result appears within the formula in italics.

▓ Click **Evaluate** again to see the result of the next underlined section and so on.

▓ When you have evaluated the whole formula, click the **Close** button to end the evaluation or the **Restart** button (that replaces the **Evaluate** button) to perform the evaluation again.

⇨ *If the formula you are evaluating contains a reference to another formula, the **Step In** button shows the detail of that formula, when it is underlined, in a new part of the evaluation box. The **Step Out** button returns to the initial formula.*

E-Using the Watch Window toolbar

*The **Watch Window** toolbar allows you to see cell contents and details of formulas, without those cells being necessarily on the screen.*

▓ Select the cells you wish to examine.

▓ **Tools**
Formula Auditing  on the **Formula Auditing** toolbar
Show Watch Window

▓ Click **Add Watch**.

▓ If necessary, modify the selection and click the **Add** button.

*As long as the **Watch Window** toolbar is displayed, you can select a new cell (or range) at any time and add it to the list of watched items.*

click to close the **Watch Window**

Book	Sheet	Name	Cell	Value	Formula
Joe's Bottle Shop.xls	Orders...		D39	2,556.60	=SUM(D3:D38)
Joe's Bottle Shop.xls	Orders...		E38	383.49	=IF(D39>2000,D39*15%,D39*20%)
Joe's Bottle Shop.xls	Orders...	Total_June	E53	0	=SUM(E47:E52)

⇨ *You can change the column widths on the **Watch Window** toolbar by dragging the vertical line between the column headers.*

⇨ *To go rapidly to a cell listed in the **Watch Window** toolbar, double-click that cell's row in the list.*

⇨ *To select all the cells containing formulas in order to add them to the **Watch Window** toolbar, use the **Edit - Go To** command, click the **Special** button and choose **Formulas**.*

F-Tracing the relationships between formulas and cells

Showing precedent cells

These are the cells which are involved in the calculation formula.

▓ Activate the cell containing the formula then select **Tools - Formula Auditing - Trace Precedents** (or click ⊞ on the **Formula Auditing** toolbar).

⇨ *To clear the auditing arrows, use the **Tools - Formula Auditing - Remove All Arrows** command or the ⊞ tool button.*

Showing dependent cells

Dependent cells are those that contain formulas that refer to the selected cell. Like precedents, they can be highlighted with arrows.

▓ Activate the cell concerned then select **Tools - Formula Auditing - Trace Dependents** (or click the ⊞ tool button on the **Formula Auditing** toolbar).

⇨ *To clear the auditing arrows, use the **Tools - Formula Auditing - Remove All Arrows** command or the ⊞ tool button (on the **Formula Auditing** toolbar).*

CALCULATION

5.1 Rows, columns and cells

A-Inserting rows/columns

▓ Select the entire row (or the entire column) after which you wish to insert the new row/column. You can select a row or column by clicking its header.

▓ Point to the fill handle, hold down the `⇧ Shift` key and drag the fill handle downwards (for rows) or to the right (for columns) to cover as many rows or columns as you want to insert.

▓ Release the mouse button followed by the `⇧ Shift` key.

⇨ *When you insert a row or column, the inserted item adopts the formatting of the row or column previously located there. You can modify this by clicking the Insert Options button that appears next to the inserted item. In the menu that appears. Choose to Format Same As Above or Format Same As Below (for a row), to Format Same As Right or Format Same As Left (for a column) or to Clear Formatting altogether.*

⇨ *The Insert - Rows or Insert - Columns command allows you to insert before the selected row or column.*

⇨ *You can also insert a row or column by selecting a row or column (click its header) and pressing* `Ctrl` *+.*

B-Deleting rows/columns

▓ Select the rows (or columns) you wish to delete, by clicking their headers.

▓ Point to the fill handle, hold down the `⇧ Shift` key and drag the fill handle downwards (for rows) or to the right (for columns) to cover as many rows or columns as you want to delete.

▓ Release the mouse button followed by the `⇧ Shift` key.

⇨ *Use Edit - Delete to delete your selection.*

C-Modifying the width of a column/height of a row

▓ Select each column to be resized to the same width (or each row to be given the same new height); if only one column or row is concerned, you do not need to select it.

▓ Point to the vertical line on the right of one of the selected columns (or to the horizontal line under the row number).

▓ Drag the line to resize the column or row.

⇨ *You can adjust the width of a column or the height of a row to fit its widest or tallest cell entry. To do this, double-click the vertical line to the right of the letter, to adjust the width of a column, or double-click the horizontal line beneath the number, to adjust the height of a row.*

D-Moving and inserting cells/rows/columns

▓ Select the cells, rows or columns to be moved.

▓ Point to one edge of the selected range then holding the ⌈⇧ Shift⌉ key down, drag the selection into position.

▓ Release the mouse when the insertion point (displayed as a thick grey line) is correctly placed.

Excel moves the cells (or rows or columns), inserting them between the existing cells (or rows or columns).

⇨ *Holding down* ⌈Ctrl⌉ *as well as* ⌈⇧ Shift⌉ *when you drag a selection, moves a copy of the cells, rows or columns instead of the original item.*

E-Inserting/deleting cells

▓ Select as many cells as you are going to insert.

▓ **Insert - Cells**
or right-click the selection and choose **Insert**.

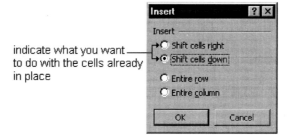

indicate what you want
to do with the cells already
in place

▓ Click **OK**.

⇨ *To delete the selected cells, use **Edit - Delete** then choose to **Shift cells left** or to **Shift cells up**.*

PRESENTATION

5.2 Formatting

A-Applying an automatic format to a table

▦ Select the table to be formatted then use **Format** - **AutoFormat**.

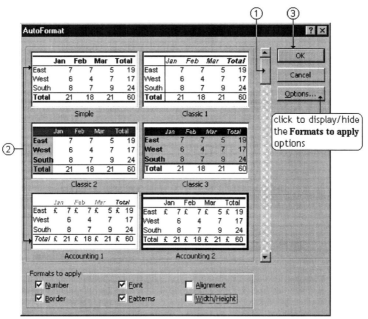

① Drag the scroll box to display the required format.
② Select the format.
③ Apply the format.

B-Formatting numerical values

▦ Select the values concerned then choose one of the number formats from the **Formatting** toolbar:

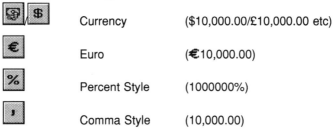

	Currency	($10,000.00/£10,000.00 etc)
	Euro	(€10,000.00)
	Percent Style	(1000000%)
	Comma Style	(10,000.00)

⇨ *Number symbols (#) may appear if a cell's width is insufficient. Once the format has been applied you could increase the column width, as necessary.*

⇨ *To change the default currency symbol, open the Windows **Control Panel** (on your Desktop, double-click **My Computer** then double-click **Control Panel**) then double-click **Regional Options** (or **Regional Settings**) select the **Currency** tab and choose the required **Currency symbol**.*

⇨ *If necessary, click the 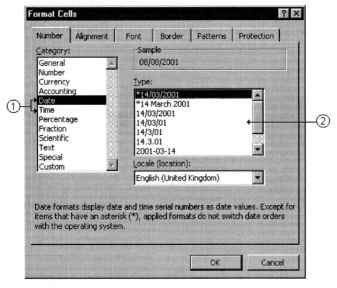 tool button to show one more decimal place or ▒ to show one less. Other formats are available in the **Format Cells** dialog box (**Format - Cells**).*

C-Formatting dates/times

▒ Select the dates to be formatted then use **Format - Cells** or Ctrl 1
▒ If necessary, activate the **Number** tab.

① Choose the **Date** or **Time** category.
② Select the format.

D-Creating a custom format

▒ Select the cells to which you want to apply the format.
▒ **Format - Cells** or Ctrl 1 - **Number** tab

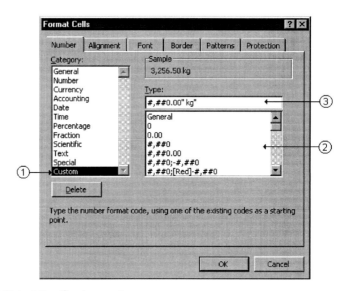

① Select the **Custom** category.

② Choose the format closest to what you have in mind.

③ Enter your custom format.

⇨ *When text is being added to a format, it must be entered between quotation marks.*

⇨ *Use the @ character to represent the cell contents, when the cell contains text.*

⇨ *For hiding cell contents, create a format ;;; (three semi-colons).*

E- Creating a conditional format

▨ Select the cells concerned.

▨ **Format - Conditional Formatting**

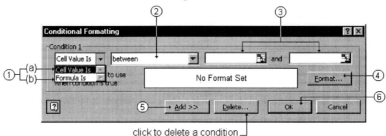

click to delete a condition

① Indicate whether:

    (a)   the condition applies to a value contained in the selected cells

    (b)   the condition applies to a formula.

② If you have chosen (a), select an operator of comparison. If you have chosen (b), give the formula.

③ If necessary, give the value(s) with which to compare the value in each cell.

④ Define the format which will be applied to the cells if the condition is met then click **OK** in the **Format Cells** dialog box.

⑤ Define additional formats if you need to.

⑥ Create the format(s).

F- Modifying the orientation of a text

▓ Select the cells concerned.

▓ **Format - Cells** or ⌨ 1

▓ Under the **Alignment** tab, choose **Orientation**:

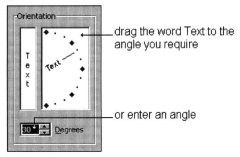

drag the word Text to the angle you require

or enter an angle

G-Aligning cell contents

⌐🖑▓ Select the cells concerned then click ▤ left alignment, ▤ centered or ▤ right alignment.

▤▓ **Format - Cells** or ⌨ 1 - **Alignment** tab

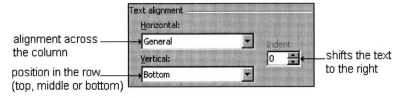

alignment across the column

position in the row (top, middle or bottom)

shifts the text to the right

⇨ *To centre cell contents across several columns, select the cells across which the text should be centred (the first cell in the range must contain the text) and click* ▦. *This centres the text and merges the cells. To undo the cell merge, click this tool button again.*

H-Adjusting row height to text

▓ Activate the cell required or select the cells concerned.

▓ **Format - Cells** or ⌘ **1** - **Alignment** tab

▓ Activate the **Wrap text** option.

I- Modifying the font/size/colour of the characters

▓ Select the cells or characters concerned then choose the font, size and colour from the list boxes on the **Formatting** toolbar.

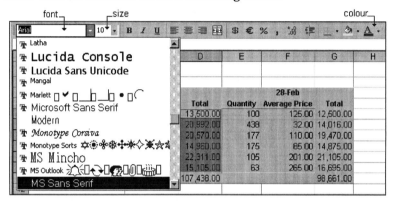

⇨ *To redefine the default font and font size used in a workbook, use* **Tools - Options - General** *tab. Define the new* **Standard Font** *and* **Size**. *These modifications will take effect when you next start Excel.*

J- Adjusting the size of characters automatically

▓ Select the cells concerned then use **Format - Cells** or ⌘ **1** - **Alignment** tab.

▓ Activate the **Shrink to fit** option.

▓ Click **OK**.

⇨ *Characters which have been reduced in size return to their original size if you widen the column.*

K-Formatting characters

▓ Select the cells or characters concerned then activate the attribute(s) you want to apply:

B	⌘ B	**bold**
I	⌘ I	*italic*
U	⌘ U	underlined

⇨ *If you repeat the same action for the same text, you cancel the corresponding attribute.*

Select the cells or characters concerned then use **Format** - **Cells** or Ctrl **1** - **Font** tab.

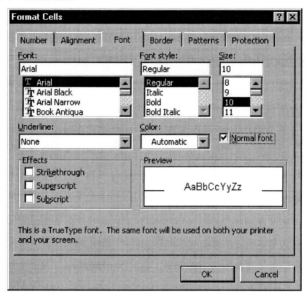

Activate all the formats to be applied to the text.

L-Drawing borders around cells

Applying borders

Select the cells concerned then choose a border from the palette on the **Formatting** toolbar:

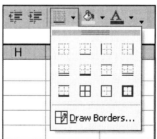

Select the cells concerned and use **Format** - **Cells** or [Ctrl] **1** - **Border** tab.

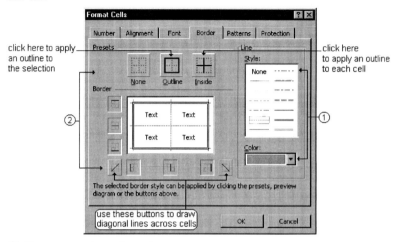

click here to apply an outline to the selection

click here to apply an outline to each cell

use these buttons to draw diagonal lines across cells

① Choose a style and a colour.

② Indicate the position of the lines making up the border.

Drawing borders

▨ Open the [ ] list by clicking the black arrow then click the **Draw Borders** option.

▨ The **Borders** toolbar appears and the pointer takes the shape of a pencil:

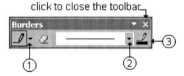

click to close the toolbar

① The default drawing mode is **Draw Border** which draws an outline around the selected area. If you wish to draw inside gridlines instead, open this list and choose the **Draw Border Grid** option.

When you choose **Draw Border Grid** mode, the pencil pointer is accompanied by a small grid.

② If required, open this list and choose a line style.

③ Click if you want to select another colour.

▨ To draw a border along one edge of a range of cells, drag along that edge.

▨ To draw a border around the outside of a range or a grid within a range, drag from the starting cell up to the last cell required.

	A	B	C	D	E	F	G	H
1								
2	Orders 14 June							
3					Borders			
4								
5		Quantity	Unit Price	Total				
6	Red & Black Whisky	9	14.50	130.50				
7	Bordeaux 1999 Red	2	3.20	6.40				
8	Queen's Gin	4	11.00	44.00				
9	Wild Chicken Bourbon	5	11.60	58.00				
10	Smirchoff Vodka	8	19.50	156.00				
11	White Vermouth	4	7.80	31.20				
12								
13								

▓ To remove one or more borders, click the [⌫] tool button (the pointer becomes an eraser) and drag along the borders you wish to erase.

▓ To deactivate the border drawing mode, press [Esc] or click [✎] or [✎⊞] again.

⇨ *While you are using **Draw Border** mode, you can temporarily switch to **Draw Border Grid** mode by holding down the* [Ctrl] *key. Holding down the* [⇧ Shift] *key switches to erasing mode, with the pointer becoming an eraser temporarily.*

M- Applying colour/patterns to cells

🖰 ▓ Select the cells that you want to colour then open the [🪣▾] list and choose a colour.

🖻 ▓ Select the cells that you want to colour or shade then use **Format - Cells** or [Ctrl] 1 - **Patterns** tab.

▓ Choose a **Color** and a **Pattern**.

N-Merging cells

▓ Select the cells concerned (only the data in the first cell of the selection will appear in the merged cells).

▓ **Format - Cells** or [Ctrl] 1 - **Alignment** tab

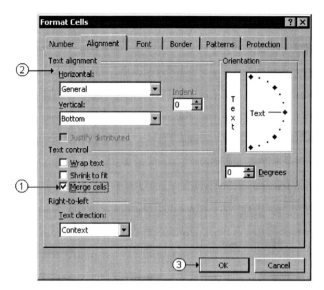

① Activate this option.

② If necessary, specify the alignment that you wish to apply to the data.

③ Click to confirm.

⇨ *The ▦ tool button merges selected cells and centres the data horizontally in the merged cells. If more than one of these cells contains data, Excel will only retain the contents of the cell on the far left.*

5.3 Styles and templates

A-Creating a style

A style is a way of saving a collection of attributes that you can then apply to other cells more quickly.

▦ Activate the cell whose formatting is to be saved as a style.

▦ **Format - Style** or ⟨Alt⟩ '

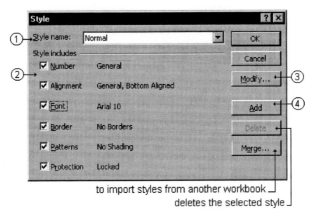

to import styles from another workbook ⌐
deletes the selected style ⌐

① Give a name for the new style.
② Deactivate any attributes you do not require.
③ If you need to, make changes to the formatting.
④ Create the style.

B-Applying a style

▦ Select the cells to be formatted.
▦ **Format** - **Style** or [Alt] '
▦ Select the style you want to use in the **Style name** list and click **OK**.

C-Creating a template

▦ Set up the workbook template, adding any elements you want workbooks created from this template to have. If required, activate worksheet or cell protection.
▦ **File - Save As**

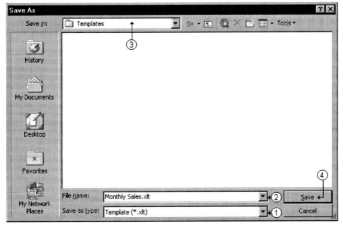

PRESENTATION

① Choose the **Template (*.xlt)** option.
② Give the new template a name.
③ If necessary, select another folder or a subfolder of **Templates**.
④ Save the template.

⇨ *Template files have an .XLT extension.*

⇨ *You can also download new workbook templates: use the **Task Pane - New Workbook - New from template** then use links: **Templates on my Web Sites** and **Templates on Microsoft.com** (View - Task Pane).*

⇨ *You cannot modify Excel built-in templates (for information, these templates reside in the folder C:\Program Files\Microsoft Office\Templates\1036, by default).*

D-Modifying a template

▦ **File - Open**

▦ Open the **Files of type** drop-down list and choose the option **Templates (*.xlt)**.

▦ Using the **Look in** list, select the folder that contains the template (by default, templates reside in C:\Windows\Application Data\Microsoft\Templates on Windows 98 and Windows ME and in C:\Documents and Settings\username\Application Data\Microsoft\Templates on Windows 2000 Professional).

▦ Double click the template you want to open.

▦ Modify your template as necessary then click ▦ to save it.

▦ Close your template.

▦ 5.4 Outlines

A-Creating the outline of a table

An outline is a way of viewing or printing the main results of a table, without looking at unnecessary detail.

Automatically

▦ Select the table concerned.

▦ **Data - Group and Outline - Auto Outline**

Manually

▨ Select the rows (or columns) that you do not need to see.

▨ **Data - Group and Outline - Group**

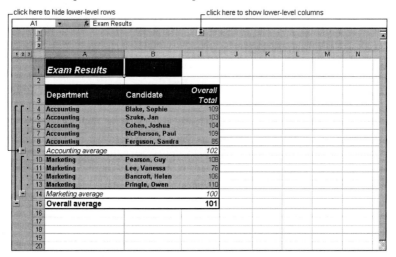

⇨ *Use the **Group** or **Ungroup** commands in the **Data - Group and Outline** menu to add or remove a row or column from the outline.*

B-Removing an outline

▨ Select the table concerned.

▨ **Data - Group and Outline - Clear Outline**

6.1 Printing

A-Printing a sheet

Activate the sheet to be printed then click the ![tool] tool.

B-Setting options for printing

File - Print or Ctrl P

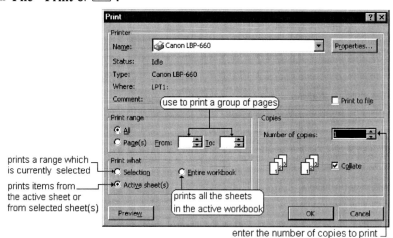

prints a range which is currently selected

prints items from the active sheet or from selected sheet(s)

use to print a group of pages

prints all the sheets in the active workbook

enter the number of copies to print

➪ If you are printing several copies of a multiple page document, the Collate option prints one complete copy of the document after another.

➪ You can also access the Print dialog box by clicking the Print button or click the Print button in Print Preview when you are in the Print Preview window.

➪ If what you are printing is several pages wide or high, you can choose how to print these pages by using the Down, then over or Over, then down options in the Page order frame in File - Page Setup - Sheet tab.

C-Creating a print area

You can define the part of the sheet you want to print as a print area.

Select the range to be printed.

File - Print Area - Set Print Area

➪ Excel keeps the last print area created in memory.

➪ To delete the print area, use File - Print Area - Clear Print Area.

D-Managing page breaks

▦ Activate the cell which is going to be the first of your new page.

▦ **Insert - Page Break**

	A	B	E	F	G
16					
17	Results Published on	09/10/01		← the page break is represented by a dotted line	
18					
19	Department	Candidate	Financial management	Sub-total	Result
20	Accounts	Barnes G.	15	40	Pass
21	Accounts	Bonino S.	12	40	Pass

⇨ *To delete the page break, activate a cell in the next row or column and use* **Insert - Remove Page Break.**

⇨ *The command* **View - Page Break Preview** *makes the page breaks visible as blue lines on the worksheet. To move a page break, drag the blue line representing it.*

E-Repeating titles on each page

▦ **File - Page Setup - Sheet** tab

▦ Activate the **Rows to Repeat at Top** box then select the rows and/or activate **Columns to Repeat at Left** and select the columns.

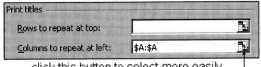

Print titles
Rows to repeat at top:
Columns to repeat at left: $A:$A

click this button to select more easily⏎

F-Previewing a printed sheet

Displaying the Print Preview

▦ **File - Print Preview** or ◪

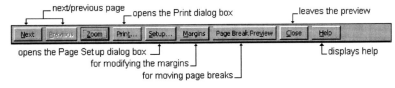

next/previous page — opens the Print dialog box — leaves the preview

| Next | Previous | Zoom | Print... | Setup... | Margins | Page Break Preview | Close | Help |

opens the Page Setup dialog box ⏌ ⏌ displays help
for modifying the margins ⏌
for moving page breaks ⏌

Print Preview buttons

▦ To zoom in on a preview, place the mouse pointer on the item to be magnified and click. Click again to return to a smaller scale.

To change the width of margins and columns widths, click the **Margins** button.

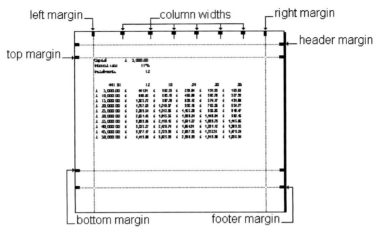

left margin column widths right margin

header margin

top margin

bottom margin footer margin

Drag the appropriate handle.

6.2 Page setup

A-Modifying page setup options

File - **Page Setup** or click the **Setup** button in the Print Preview.

Activate the **Margins** tab to define the margins.

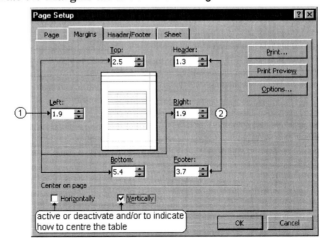

① Set the margins for printing.

② Set the positions of the header and footer.

▓ Modify the **Scaling** options under the **Page** tab:

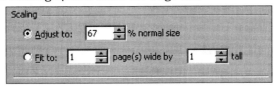

▓ Choose the appropriate **Orientation** under the **Page** tab:

▓ Set the **Print** options under the sheet tab:

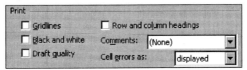

B-Creating headers and footers

▓ **File - Page Setup** or click the **Setup** button in the Print Preview **Header/Footer** tab

You could also use the command **View - Header/Footer**.

▓ Click the **Custom Header** or **Custom Footer** button in the **Page Setup** dialog box.

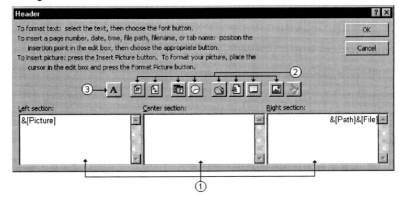

① Enter the text to be printed in the box which corresponds to the position on the page where you want the header/footer to appear. To create a second (third...) line of text, press Enter .

② To insert variable details click the appropriate buttons.

[#]	Page number	[icon]	Workbook name and file path
[icon]	Total number of pages	[icon]	Name of the workbook
[icon]	Date of printing	[icon]	Name of the sheet
[clock]	Time of printing	[icon]	Picture

③ Format the text.

⇨ *Lists of popular headers and footers are also available under the* **Header/Footer** *tab (if you select a header/footer from the list, it is automatically centred on the page).*

6.3 Working with views

A view is a way of saving certain settings, such as a print area, page setup, filter settings or hidden rows/columns. When you switch to a view, the saved options are activated automatically.

Creating a view

▓ Prepare the sheet for printing (page setup, print area, hiding columns, etc).

▓ **View - Custom Views - Add**

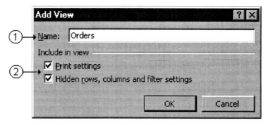

① Enter the name of the view being created.

② Indicate the elements which should be included in the view.

Using a view

▓ View - Custom Views

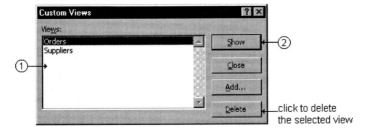

① Select the view.
② Activate the view.

PRINTING

7.1 Creating a chart

A- Creating a chart

▓ Select the cells that contain the data needed for the chart.

▓ If the data for the chart is in several different ranges, select the non-adjacent ranges in the usual way (with Ctrl-clicks). Make sure the cell ranges selected form a coherent set each time, including blank cells if necessary.

	A	B	C	D
1		JANUARY	FEBRUARY	MARCH
2	PETER	4,568.90	3,958.00	4,578.50
3	CALLUM	2,587.00	3,250.00	2,356.00
4	SUE	6,589.10	3,845.00	4,578.90
5	JOSH	6,348.00	7,890.00	7,845.10
6	ANNE	2,890.00	4,560.00	3,589.00
7	WENDY	4,578.90	7,125.00	4,560.00
8	BEN	3,875.00	4,500.00	5,230.00
9	PHILIP	4,580.00	5,845.00	2,356.00

Excel considers the selected ranges as one rectangular block

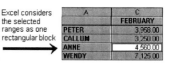

In the example above, the blank cell in the top left corner was included to ensure a symmetrical selection.

▓ **Insert - Chart** or ▣

▓ Select the **Chart type** and then the **Chart sub-type** then click the **Next** button.

▓ Check the references of the selected cells in the **Data range** box and if necessary, modify the selection using the ▣ button.
Indicate whether the series are in rows or columns (**Rows** or **Columns** option).

If the chart shown does not resemble the required chart, click the **Series** tab to check the references of each series.

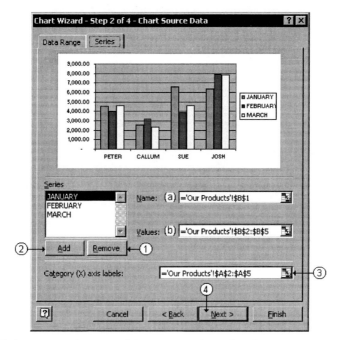

① Delete any series you wish to remove from the chart

② To add a series, click the button, give its name (a), then give the references of the cells containing the values for the series (b).

③ Specify the range of cells which contains the text for the category (X) axis labels or type the text.

④ Go on to the next step.

▨ Customise your chart by giving the various chart titles on the **Titles** page. At this stage in the wizard, you can also select options from the other tabs (cf. below).

▨ Click **Next**.

▨ Click **Finish**.

⇨ *In you chose to insert the chart into a worksheet, it appears in the workspace. Square black handles show that it is selected. This type of chart is known as an **embedded chart**: it belongs to the family of drawing objects.*

⇨ *To activate an embedded chart, click it once: this selects the whole object (the* **Data** *menu is replaced by the* **Chart** *menu). To deactivate it, click a cell in the sheet, outside the chart.*

⇨ *To move an embedded chart, activate it then drag it to its new position.*

⇨ *To display an embedded chart in a window, select it then use* **View - Chart Window**. *To deactivate the chart, close the window.*

B-Selecting different objects in a chart

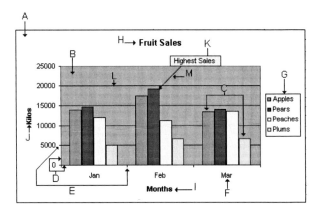

	object	how to select it
A	Chart area	click in the chart but not in any object.
B	Plot area	click in the plot area but not in any object.
C	Point	click the series then click the point.
	Series	click one of the data markers in the series.
D	Value axis Category axis	click one of the tick mark labels.
E	Tick marks	no selection.
F	Tick mark labels	
G	Legend	click the object.
H	Chart title	
I	Axis title	
J	Axis title	
K	Text box	
L	Gridlines	click one of the lines.
M	Arrow	click the object.

⇨ When you point to a chart object, its name and if appropriate, its value appear in a ScreenTip, providing the **Show names** and **Show values** options are active in the **Options** dialog box *(Tools - Options - Chart* tab).

⇨ To access a dialog box in which you can format a chart object, select the object then use the first command in the **Format** menu. This command name changes depending on the object. You can also double-click the selected item.

⇨ Another way to select a chart object is to open the **Chart Objects** list box on the **Chart** toolbar and click its name.

C-Setting up the chart for printing

▨ Select the chart.

▨ **File - Page Setup**

▨ As well as modifying the usual options, you can adjust the **Printed Chart Size** under the **Chart** tab.

7.2 Chart options

A-Changing the chart type

▨ Activate the chart.

▨ **Chart - Chart Type**

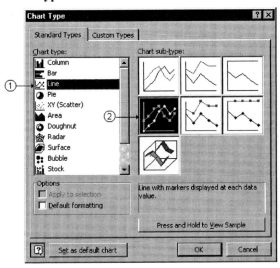

① Choose the chart type.

② Double-click the sub-type you prefer.

⇨ *You can use the* *button on the Chart toolbar to change the chart type but not to choose from the various sub-types.*

⇨ *If you need to redefine one or more of the chart's series, take the Source Data option in the Chart menu.*

⇨ *All the options for managing the chart can be found in Chart - Chart Options.*

B-Displaying the data table

Under the chart, you can display the table of data on which it is based.

▓ **Chart - Chart Options - Data Table** tab

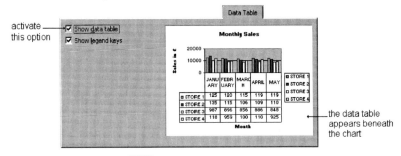

activate this option

the data table appears beneath the chart

⇨ *You can also click the* ▦ *tool button on the Chart toolbar.*

C-Managing pie charts

Rotating a pie chart

▓ Select the series.

▓ **Format**
Selected Data Series
Options tab   `Ctrl` **1**

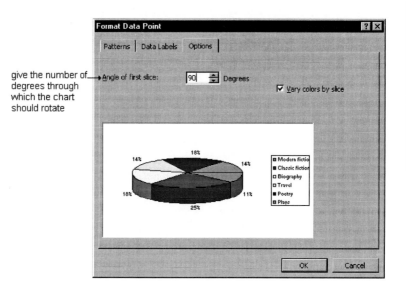

give the number of degrees through which the chart should rotate

Exploding a slice

Select the slice you want to explode and drag it away from the rest.

D-Inserting gridlines in a chart

Chart - Chart Options - Gridlines tab

vertical gridlines

horizontal gridlines

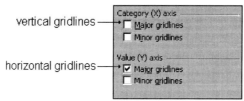

E-Changing the scale of the chart

Select the value axis.

Format
Selected Axis
Scale tab

Ctrl 1

Set the scale options:

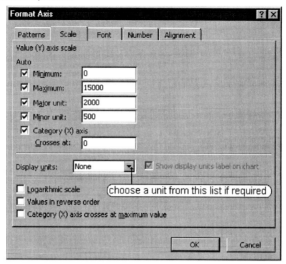

F-Modifying the display of tick marks and their labels

Select the axis on which the tick mark labels need formatting.

Format
Selected Axis

Ctrl 1

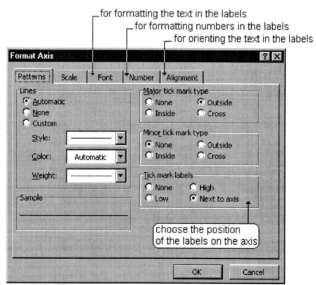

⇨ *With the* *and* buttons on the **Chart** toolbar you can also change the orientation of the text in the labels.*

G-Modifying the content of the category labels

▦ **Chart** - **Source Data** - **Series** tab
▦ Change the contents of the **Category (X) axis labels** box.
▦ Click **OK**.

H-Making bars overlap

▦ Select one of the series in the chart.
▦ **Format**   Ctrl 1
Selected Data Series
Options tab

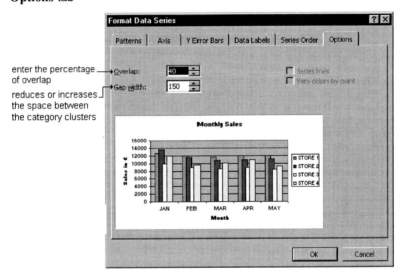

enter the percentage of overlap

reduces or increases the space between the category clusters

I- Linking points in a line chart

▦ Select a series.
▦ **Format**   Ctrl 1
Selected Data Series
Options tab

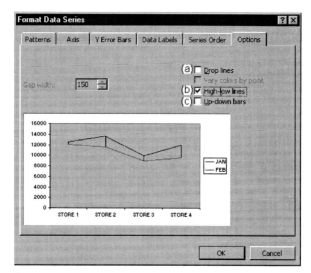

■ Choose between:

  (a)   to link points to the category axis.
  (b)   to link point to point.
  (c)   to use bars to link the points.

J- Adjusting the display of data in 3D charts

■ Chart - 3-D View

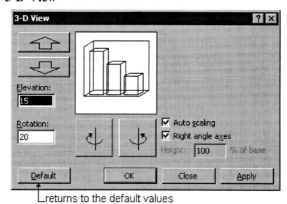

└─returns to the default values

K-Changing the chart depth

■ Select a data series in your 3D chart.

■ **Format**   1
  Selected Data Series
  Options tab

- In the **Chart depth** box enter a value between 20 and 2000.
- Click **OK**.

L- Creating a custom chart

- Select the chart which will be used as a model.
- **Chart - Chart Type - Custom Types** tab
- Activate the **User-defined** option in the **Select from** list.
- Click **Add**.
- Fill in your chart **Name** and **Description** in the **Add Custom Chart Type** dialog box.
- Click **OK** twice.

M-Using a custom chart

- Select the data you want to show as a chart.
- **Insert - Chart - Custom Types** tab
- Activate the **User-defined** open in the **Select from** frame.
- Double-click the **Chart type** which interests you.
- Select or enter the range of data that you want the chart to represent in the **Data Range** box, then specify if the data is in **Rows** or **Columns**.
- Click **Next**.
- Under the **Titles** tab, specify your **Chart title** and the title of the axes.
- Specify, if necessary, where you want to place the legend, under the **Legend** tab.
- Click **Next**.
- Choose where the chart will be placed and click **Finish**.

N-Formatting characters in a chart object

- Select the drawing object which contains the text.
- Use the various tool buttons on the **Formatting** toolbar or, if these do not correspond to your needs, open the **Format [object]** dialog box using the **Format - [name of object]** command or the 🔲 tool button and use the formatting options provided.

⇨ *The format of numerical values in the chart is defined in the same way.*

O-Changing the border/colour/shading of a chart object

- Select the element you want to modify.
- **Format**   double-click the object   Ctrl 1
  Selected [object]

For unattached text, double-click one of the selection borders, which will open the Format [name of object] dialog box.

▨ If necessary, activate the **Patterns** tab.

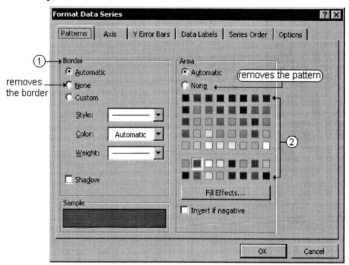

① Choose a border.

② Choose a background colour.

▨ To apply a pattern or a texture to the object, click the **Fill Effects** button.

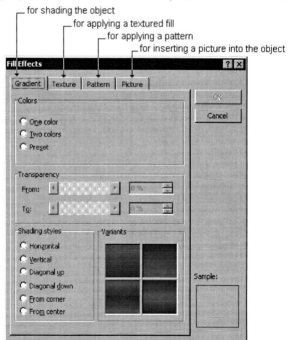

P-Managing chart objects

▓ To move or resize an object, select it and drag one of the selection handles to change its dimensions, or one of the borders to move it.

▓ To delete an object, select it and press ⌷Del⌷ or use the **Edit - Clear - All** commands.

Q-Adding text to a chart

A title

▓ **Chart - Chart Options -Titles** tab

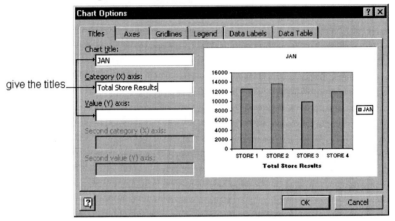

give the titles

A text linked to one or more points in a series

▓ Select the point or series concerned.

▓ **Format**
Selected Data
or **Selected Data Series**
Data Labels tab

 ⌷Ctrl⌷ 1

① Activate the options of your choice.

② If you choose several options, select the type of separator to display between each value.

Unattached text (text box)

▨ Make sure that you have not selected any text objects.

▨ Type the text required and press Enter .

⇨ *The drawing object created is named Text Box.*

⇨ *To edit the text, select the object (if it is a title or data label), click in the text, modify it and press* Esc .

⇨ *To delete a text box, select it then press* Del .

⇨ *To enter different types of text on several lines, press* Ctrl Enter *every time you change lines.*

R-Inserting a text from a sheet into a chart

▨ Make sure that you have not selected any chart object containing text.

▨ Type =

▨ Select the cell(s) containing the text to be inserted and enter.

▨ Drag the text box to where you want it.

⇨ *Each time the contents of the cells from the worksheet change, this text will be updated.*

S-Managing the legend

▨ If necessary, activate the chart then use **Chart - Chart Options - Legend** tab.

▨ To display or hide the legend, activate or deactivate the **Show legend** option.

▨ If required, choose the legend's **Placement** (position) in relation to the chart.

▨ Click **OK**.

⇨ *You can also show or hide the legend with the* 🔲 *tool button on the* **Chart** *toolbar.*

⇨ *The legend can also be dragged to its new position.*

T-Adding/deleting a category in an embedded chart

▨ Select the chart area.

🖱▨ To add a new category and its corresponding data points, drag the handle of the purple rectangle until it encompasses the cells containing the new category. To delete a category, reduce the rectangle so the data in question is excluded from it.

⇨ *If the category you wish to add is not adjacent to the existing categories, you can select the corresponding cells and drag them into the chart.*

▤▨ Select the chart area then use **Chart - Add Data**.

▓ In the **Range** text box, give the references of the data you want to add then click **OK**.

*If the **Paste Special** dialog box appears, activate the **New point(s)** option. In the **Values (Y) in** frame, indicate whether the series are in rows or columns. Activate the **Categories (X Labels) in First Column** option if the selected range contains category labels.*

▓ Click **OK**.

U-Modifying the chart type for a data series

▓ Select the series concerned then use **Chart - Chart Type**

▓ Select the required **Chart type** and **Chart sub-type**.

▓ Make sure the **Apply to selection** option is active.

▓ Click **OK**.

▓ If you wish, modify the presentation of this series by making sure the series is still selected and using **Format - Selected Data Series**.

V-Adding a secondary axis

▓ Select the series concerned then choose **Format - Selected Data Series - Axis** tab.

▓ Activate the **Secondary axis** option then click **OK**.

W- Adding/deleting a data series in an embedded chart

▓ To add a data series select the chart area (the cells containing the data series are enclosed in a green rectangle) and drag the handle of the green rectangle until it has encompassed the values of the new series. If the chart is in a chart sheet, you can copy the source data using the clipboard.

▓ To delete a data series, choose **Chart - Source Data - Series** tab, select the **Series** and click the **Remove** button.

X-Changing the order of the series

▓ Select one of the series on the chart.

▓ **Format**   Ctrl 1
  Selected Data Series
  Series Order tab

① Click the series you wish to move.

② Click one of these buttons to move the series up or down the order.

Y- Unlinking a chart from the worksheet

▓ For each data series:
- select the series,
- select everything that appears in the formula bar,
- press ⌨F9 and enter.

7.3 Drawing objects

A- Drawing an object

▓ Display the **Drawing** toolbar ().

▓ Click the tool button corresponding to the shape you want to draw (the appendix includes a description of the **Drawing** toolbar) or click the **AutoShapes** button then choose one of the shapes proposed.

▓ Drag to draw the object. Hold down the ⌨Alt key as you drag to align the shape with the cell gridlines.

⇨ *Hold the ⌨⇧Shift key down to draw a perfect circle, square or arc, and for a perfectly straight horizontal, vertical or diagonal line.*

B- Creating a text box

A text box is a drawing object intended to contain text.

▓ Click the tool button on the **Drawing** toolbar.

▓ Drag to draw the text box or click the place you wish to start entering the text. Use the ⌨Alt key as you drag if you wish to align the text box to the cell grid.

▓ Enter your text, without worrying about line breaks. Use the ⟨Enter⟩ key when you want to start a new paragraph.

▓ Press the ⟨Esc⟩ key when you have finished.

➩ *You can go on to format the characters you have entered.*

➩ *A text box is a drawing object which can be modified using the **Drawing** toolbar tools.*

➩ *To add text to a drawing or AutoShape, right-click the drawn shape and select **Add Text**.*

C-Inserting a picture, a sound or a video clip

Finding and inserting a picture, a sound or a video clip

▓ Use the **Insert - Picture - Clip Art** command to display the **Insert Clip Art** task pane.

*The **Add Clips to Organizer** dialog box may appear on the screen:*

*If the dialog box illustrated above appears, click the **Now** button if you want to add the image, audio and video files from your hard disk or another source into the Clip Organizer (if you do not want to do that just yet, click the **Later** button).*

① Enter one or more keywords.

② Define where the search should be carried out by selecting (or dese-lecting) the corresponding categories.

The **Office Collections** category and its subcategories correspond to the image, sound and video elements installed with Office. The **Web Collections** category provides you with elements found on the Web (or more precisely on the Microsoft site). Excel will take this category into account only if you have an open Internet connection.

③ If necessary, limit the type of items included in the search (**Clip Art, Photographs, Movies** or **Sounds**), by selecting or deselecting these elements as required.

④ Start the search.

If you want to interrupt the search, click the **Stop** button that appears near the bottom of the pane.

▦ When the search is finished or if you click the **Stop** button, the **Modify** button appears, which you can use to set up a new search.

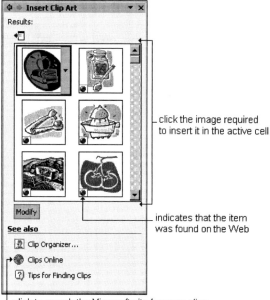

click the image required to insert it in the active cell

indicates that the item was found on the Web

click to search the Microsoft site for more clips

▦ To work with an item, point to it and click the arrow that appears to the right of it.

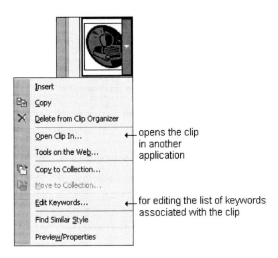

opens the clip
in another
application

for editing the list of keywords
associated with the clip

Using the Clip Organizer

▓ If necessary, display the **Insert - Clip Art** task pane (using the **Insert Picture - Clip Art** command, for example).

The Add Clips to Organizer dialog box may appear on the screen: in this case, click the Now button if you want to add the image, audio and video files from your hard disk or another source into the Clip Organizer, otherwise, click the Later button.

▓ Click the **Clip Organiser** link at the bottom of the task pane.

▓ If the **Add Clips to Organizer** dialog box appears again, choose to add or not to add picture, audio or video files from you hard disk to the **Clip Organizer**.

closes the organizer

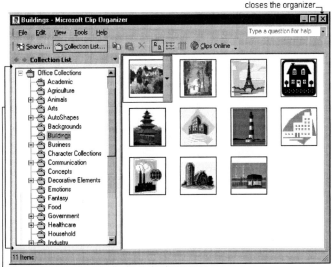

click a collection and/or subcollection to view its contents

- To create a new collection within **My Collections**, select **My Collections** then use the **File - New Collection** command and enter the new collection's **Name**. Decide where to store this new collection then click **OK**.

- To copy a picture, sound or video clip into a subcollection of **My Collections,** look for the item in the **Office Collections** or **Web Collections** (if you are connected to the Internet) then drag the item from the right pane into the required subcollection in the left pane.

- You can add a picture, sound or video clip to your document, drag the item from the right pane of the **Clip Organizer** window onto the active document.

  The Clip Organizer window disappears but is still open in the background; you can reactivate it by clicking its link on the task pane.

⇨ *To see more complex AutoShapes in the **Insert Clip Art** task pane, click the **AutoShapes** button on the **Drawing** toolbar and choose the **More AutoShapes** option.*

⇨ *To display an image in the background of a worksheet, activate the sheet then use **Format - Sheet - Background**, choose the image then click **Insert**.*

⇨ *To modify the format of a selected picture, choose **Format - Picture - Picture Size** tab and in the **Size and rotate** frame, enter the required **Height** and **Width**.*

D-Inserting a WordArt object

The WordArt application applies special effects to a text:

- Click the [button] button on the **Drawing** toolbar.
- Select an effect then click **OK**.

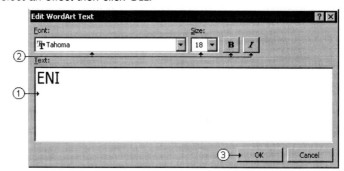

① Type in the text
② Format the text, if appropriate.
③ Create the object.

⇨ *When the text object is selected, you can edit it using the tools from the WordArt bar.*

E- Inserting a diagram

▓ Click the ⬚ tool button on the **Drawing** toolbar.

▓ Select the type of diagram you wish to use then click **OK**.

The chosen type of diagram appears in a drawing canvas and the Organization Chart toolbar appears, if you choose that type of diagram. If you choose another type, the Diagram toolbar appears.

▓ Enter your text in the **Click to add text** boxes.

▓ To add another shape to an **Organization Chart**, choose the shape to which you wish to link the new one. Open the **Insert Shape** list on the **Organization Chart** toolbar and select the type of shape you wish to add. For other types of diagram, just click the **Insert Shape** button on the **Diagram** toolbar.

▓ To delete a shape from a diagram, click the edge of the shape to select it, then press ⬚Del.

⇨ *The ⬚ tool button on the Organization Chart or Diagram toolbar applies an automatic format to the diagram.*

⇨ *To delete a diagram, click it to activate it then click its hatched border and press ⬚Del.*

F- Managing drawing objects

▓ Click ⬚ on the **Drawing** toolbar.

▓ To select several objects at once, click the first object to select it and hold down the ⬚⇧Shift key as you click each of the other objects you want to select.

▓ To delete an object, select it and press ⬚Del.

▓ To resize an object, drag one of the handles which surround it when it is selected.

▓ To move an object, point to its border and drag it. Use the ⬚Alt key as you drag to align the object with the cell grid.

▓ To group a collection of selected objects, click the **Draw** button on the **Drawing** toolbar, then click **Group**. To ungroup objects, use **Draw - Ungroup**.

▓ To change the order of overlapping objects, select the object that you want to bring forward or send further back. Click the **Draw** button then point to the **Order** option.

Choose:

(a)   to bring the object to the front.

(b)   to send the object to the back.

(c)   to bring it one place forward.

(d)   to send it one place back.

▓ To align objects with one another, select the objects concerned, click the **Draw** button then choose one of the first six options in the **Align or Distribute** menu.

▓ To rotate an object, select it then point to the small green circle at the top of the object or picture and drag to rotate the object.

G-Changing an object's appearance

A 2D object

▓ Select the object and use the buttons on the **Drawing** toolbar:

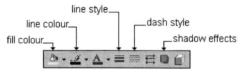

⇨ *The* *tool button is used to define arrowheads for line objects.*

⇨ *To remove an object's borders, select it then choose **Format - Text Box - Colors and Lines** tab. Go into the **Color** list and choose the **No Line** option.*

A 3D object

▓ To add a 3D effect to an object, select the object then click the [button] button on the **Drawing** toolbar to choose a preset 3D style.

To create your own 3D effect, select the object, click [button] then the **3D Settings** button.

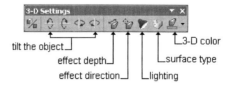

⇨ *To change the depth of a 3D chart, select the series you wish to modify, and choose* **Format - Selected Data Series**. *Activate the* **Options** *tab and modify the values of your choice.*

⇨ *To change the presentation of a 3D chart, use* **Chart - 3D View** *then enter the values of your choice in the* **Elevation, Rotation** *and* **Perspective** *text boxes or click the increment arrows.*

8.1 Working with a list of data

A-Defining data list terms

A list of data is commonly called a database.

▓ Each separate column of data constitutes a **field**.

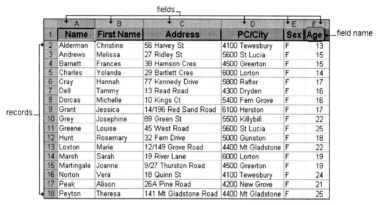

When you are creating a list of data, you can define the type of data allowed in each field by defining validation criteria.

B-Using the data form

Accessing the form

▓ Click a cell in the table that you want to manage as a database.

▓ **Data - Form**

This form is made up of the following elements:

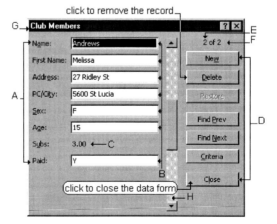

A	Field names
B	Edit boxes for entering field contents
C	Data form fields containing computed fields
D	Command buttons
E	The number of the current record
F	The total number of records
G	Title bar
H	Vertical scroll bar

C-Managing records

▓ To add a new record, click the **New** button then fill in each new record: press ⏎ to move to the next box, except after the last one; ⇧Shift ⏎ to go back to the previous box. To confirm the data entered, press Enter.

▓ To move from record to record, use the scroll bar or the arrow keys:

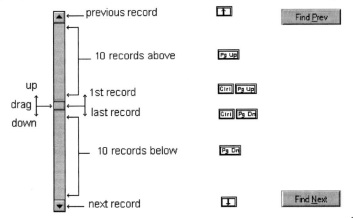

▓ To edit a record, access it, make the necessary changes then press Enter (the **Restore** button retrieves the former values).

⇨ *The last form displayed is always a new form, ready to be filled in.*

Finding a particular record

▓ Display either the first or last record.

▓ Click the **Criteria** button.

▓ Enter the search criteria in the same way as you would fill in a record but without pressing Enter.

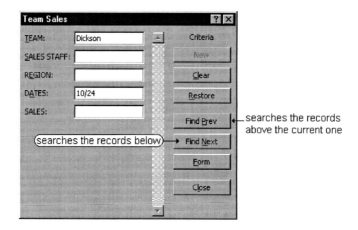

searches the records
above the current one

searches the records below

8.2 Filters

A-Creating and using a simple filter

Using a filter, you can select records corresponding to a particular criterion.

▓ **Data - Filter - AutoFilter**

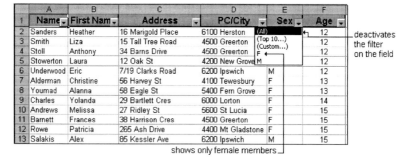

shows only female members

Each field becomes a drop-down list which opens when you click the down arrow.

▓ To filter by one of the values listed, open the list associated with the field concerned and click the value.

Filtering the highest and lowest values

▓ Open the field concerned and click (**Top 10...**).

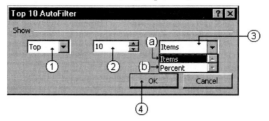

① Indicate whether you want top values or bottom values.
② Specify how many of the top/bottom values you wish to see.
③ Choose:

   (a)   to filter all the records corresponding to the criteria (top or bottom).

   (b)   to filter a number of rows corresponding to a percentage of the total number of values in the list.

④ Apply the filter.

Filtering by custom criteria

▓ Click **Custom** in the list for the field concerned.

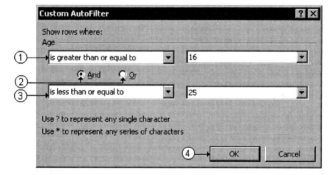

① Give the operator and the value which make up the first filter criterion.
② Choose **And** if both criteria must be satisfied together. Choose **Or** if either one or the other must be satisfied.
③ Enter the second condition.
④ Apply the filter.

⇨ *To combine criteria relating to several fields and connected with the "and" operator, enter the conditions in each field concerned.*

⇨ *To display all the records again, use the command **Data - Filter - Show All**.*

LISTS OF DATA

B-Creating and using complex filters

Creating a criteria range

▒ In a space on the worksheet, type a first row made up of the names of the fields to be used in the filter criteria. In the rows below, type the criteria:

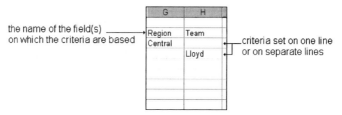

the name of the field(s) on which the criteria are based → Region / Central / Team / Lloyd ← criteria set on one line or on separate lines

▒ The criteria must be set out as follows:

Combination	Method
OR	enter the criteria in several rows
AND	enter the criteria in several columns
AND and OR	enter the criteria in several rows and several columns

The examples below will help:

Requirements	Criteria ranges	
Records concerning Central, Western and Southern regions: Central region OR Western region OR Southern region	**Region**	
	Centre	
	West	
	South	
Central Region records made by Lloyd: Central Region AND Lloyd's team	**Region**	**Team**
	Centre	Lloyd
Central Region records made by Lloyd or Allen or Carter: Central Region AND (Lloyd's team OR Allen's team OR Carter's team)	**Region**	**Team**
	Centre	Lloyd
	Centre	Allen
	Centre	Carter

⇨ *To extract MARTIN but not MARTINEZ, MARTINELLI..., enter the criteria "MARTIN".*

Using a criteria range to filter records

▓ Click inside the database and use the **Data - Filter - Advanced Filter** command.

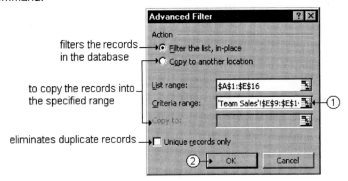

filters the records in the database

to copy the records into the specified range

eliminates duplicate records

① Click here then select the criteria range on the worksheet.
② Apply the filter.

⇨ *To copy the records which meet the filter criteria, the first row of the destination range (whose location is given in the **Copy to** box) must contain the names of the fields to filter.*

⇨ *If you change the criteria range, run the filter again.*

C-Calculating statistics from the records

▓ Create the appropriate criteria range then use the following functions:

Function	Effect
=DCOUNT(database,field,criteria)	counts the cells
=DSUM(database,field,criteria)	totals the values of the field
=DAVERAGE(database,field,criteria)	calculates the average for the field
=DMAX(database,field,criteria)	extracts the maximal value in the field
=DMIN(database,field,criteria)	extracts the minimal value in the field

database the reference of the cells containing the list of records (including column headings).

field the column heading.

criteria either the word **criteria** if you have created a complex filter or the references of the cells containing the criteria range.

⇨ *As soon as you change an item in the criteria range, Excel updates the statistics automatically.*

8.3 Pivot tables

A-Making a pivot table

A pivot table allows you to synthesise and analyse data from a list or an existing table.

▨ Click in the data list.

▨ **Data - PivotTable and PivotChart Report** or

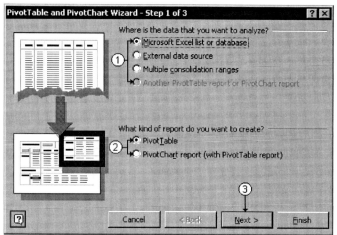

① Indicate the data source you want to analyse.

② Do you want to create just a pivot table, or a pivot table combined with a pivot chart?

③ Click to continue creating the table.

▨ If necessary, select the **Range** of cells containing the data used to fill in the table then click **Next**.

▨ Click **Layout**.

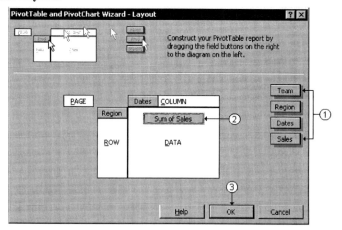

① Drag the field labels of your choice towards the corresponding location (ROW, COLUMN, PAGE, DATA) to define the layout of your table.

② Double-click a button to modify the field properties.

③ Click to continue creating the table.

- Indicate whether the pivot table should be created on a **New worksheet** or in an **Existing worksheet** then click **Finish**.

B-Modifying a pivot table

- To modify a pivot table, click inside the table and go through the procedure that you used to create it.
- Although a pivot table is linked to the data list from which it was created, it is not updated automatically. To update the data in the pivot table, click the  button on the **PivotTable** toolbar.
- To auto-format a pivot table, access the table then use **Format - AutoFormat** or . Choose the desired format by double-clicking it.
- If you double-click one of the result values in a pivot table's data area, Excel shows the details of the source data used to make the calculation on a separate worksheet.
- A field can also be added by dragging the corresponding field from the **PivotTable Field List** window onto the pivot table.
- To delete a field, drag the field concerned out of the pivot table.
- To change the presentation of pivot table:

	A	B	C
1	Average of Gross Wage	Region	
2	Age	East	North
3	18-24		998.4
4	25-31	1035.13	988.9

click to open the list of groups generated by Excel and activate or deactivate the values you want to show or hide

- Format the selected cells, in the same way as you would format cells in a worksheet.

C-Grouping numerical or date/time elements

- Click the title of the field by which you want to group the data.
- **Data - Group and Outline - Group**
- Indicate how you want to group the data.

⇨ *To undo groups, use the **Data - Group and Outline - Ungroup** command.*

8.4 Pivot charts

A- Creating a pivot chart

A pivot chart is always created in conjunction with a pivot table. This means that any modifications made to the table will be automatically made to the chart, and vice versa.

From an existing pivot table

▒ Access the pivot table you wish to use for the chart.

▒ Click the 📊 tool button on the **PivotTable** toolbar.

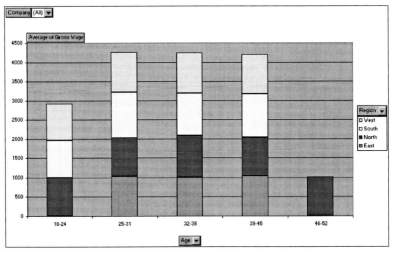

A stacked column chart appears on a separate chart sheet (stacked column is the default chart type).

The row data from the pivot table become the X-axis categories and the column data become the series.

⇨ *To modify the type of chart created, select the chart then use the 📊 button on the PivotTable toolbar.*

From a datalist

▒ Click in the datalist.

▒ **Data - Pivot Table and Pivot Chart Report** or 📊

▒ Activate the **Pivot Chart (with Pivot Table)** option then click **Next**.

▒ Indicate where the data to be analysed is located then click **Next**.

▒ Click **Layout**.

▒ To define the structure of the pivot table linked to the chart, drag the field labels of your choice onto the corresponding position on the diagram then click **OK**.

- Indicate where you want to create the pivot table; the pivot chart is, by default, created on a new worksheet.
- Click **Finish**.

⇨ *To move a pivot chart's legend, use **Chart - Chart Options - Legend** tab then choose the desired position.*

⇨ *It is not possible to move the labels of a pivot chart or those of its axes.*

⇨ *To modify the type of chart created, select the chart then use **Chart - Chart Type** and choose the desired chart type and sub-type.*

B-Hiding/showing data

- Open the list attached to the field in question, then deactivate or activate the option which corresponds to the data you want to hide or show.

C-Adding/removing a field in a pivot chart

- Drag the field button out of the chart to remove the corresponding field. To add a field, drag it from the **PivotTable Field List** onto the chart.

  *If the **PivotTable Field List** window does not appear, you can display it by clicking the ▣ tool button on the **PivotTable** toolbar.*

D-Moving a pivot chart

- Activate the worksheet containing the chart.
- **Chart - Location**

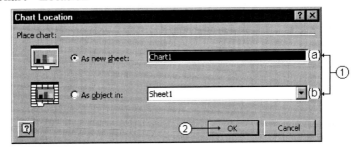

① Choose the location: (a) on a new sheet or (b) on an existing sheet.
② Click to confirm.

9.1 Protection

A-Protecting a workbook

- **File - Save As**
- If necessary, enter the name of the workbook, and specify the folder in which to save it.
- Open the **Tools** list of the dialog box and choose **General Options**.

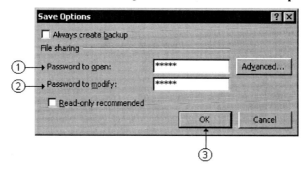

① To prevent unauthorised users from opening the workbook, type a password here.

② To allow access but prevent unauthorised modification of the document, type a password in this box.

Each character of the password is replaced by an asterisk. Excel registers the difference between capital and lower case letters: be careful which you use.

③ Click to confirm.

- Type the password again, to ensure against error, and enter.

⇨ *To delete a password, clear the corresponding text box in the Save Options dialog box.*

⇨ *The Password to open will be required as soon as a user tries to open a document. If a Password to modify has been set, a user who cannot give the password can still have access to the document by clicking the Read Only button. However in this case, if the user attempts to modify the document, Excel refuses to save the modifications.*

B-Protecting a workbook's structure and/or windows

▧ **Tools - Protect - Protect Workbook**

① Select the required options:

(a)   prevents sheets from being moved, deleted, hidden, unhidden, renamed or added.

(b)   prevents the workbook window from being moved, resized, hidden or closed.

② If you wish, set a password (up to 255 characters long).

③ Click to confirm.

▧ If you are setting a password, enter it again then click **OK**.

⇨ *To remove the protection from the workbook, use the command **Tools - Protection - Unprotect Workbook**.*

C-Limiting the cells accessible to any user

1st step: unlocking selected cells

▧ Select the cells where writing is allowed.

▧ **Format - Cells** or ⌈Ctrl⌉ 1 - **Protection** tab, deactivate the **Locked** option then enter.

2nd step: protecting the sheet

▧ **Tools - Protection - Protect Sheet**

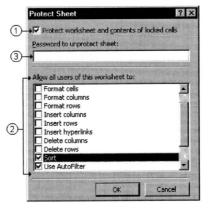

① Make sure that this option is active.

② Activate or deactivate the options to indicate which actions users can perform.

③ Enter a password or, if you are not using a password, click **OK**.

▓ Confirm your password (if you are using one) by entering it again then click **OK**.

⇨ *Depending on the user's permissions, certain options in the **Format** menu may not be available on the protected sheet (the corresponding option names will be grey).*

⇨ *To remove the protection from a sheet, use the command **Tools - Protection - Unprotect Sheet**. If necessary, give the password which protects the sheet, then enter.*

D-Giving certain users access to cells

When the cells in a sheet are protected, you can still grant access to certain ranges for certain users either by using different passwords or, if you are working under Windows 2000, by choosing the appropriate user names.

▓ **Tools - Protection - Allow Users to Edit Ranges**

▓ Click the **New** button.

① If required, change the title for the range of cells.

② Indicate the cells concerned in the worksheet.

③ Enter the password that users will have to enter to be able to modify that range.

④ Confirm then re-enter the password to confirm then click **OK** again.

▓ If you wish to define another range of cells controlled by a password, click the **New** button again and define further ranges.

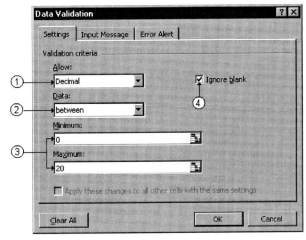

Allow Users to Edit Ranges

Ranges unlocked by a password when sheet is protected:

Title	Refers to cells
Enter Client Details	$B$2:$B$5
Enter Staff ID	$B$24

New...
Modify...
Delete

☐ Paste permissions information into a new workbook

Protect Sheet... | OK | Cancel | Apply

*A **Permissions** button appears if you are using Windows 2000. This button provides you with a list of users so you can define who can modify the range selected previously in the dialog box. This dispenses with the use of passwords.*

▓ Click the **Protect Sheet** button, make sure the **Protect worksheet and contents of locked cells** option is active and if necessary, tick any options required in the **Allow all users of this worksheet to** list.

▓ Click **OK**.

⇨ *The **Paste permissions information into a new workbook** option in the **Allow Users to Edit Ranges** dialog box makes a report of the permissions defined in a new workbook.*

E-Defining authorised data

▓ Select the cell(s) concerned.

▓ **Data - Validation - Settings** tab

Data Validation

Settings | Input Message | Error Alert

Validation criteria

① Allow:
Decimal ☑ Ignore blank

② Data:
between ④

③ Minimum:
0

Maximum:
20

☐ Apply these changes to all other cells with the same settings

Clear All | OK | Cancel

① Choose the type of data you wish to authorise.

② Choose a comparison operator.

③ Give values for comparison.

④ Activate this option if you authorise the cell to remain empty.

▦ Click **OK**.

⇨ *Data entered before the criteria were set are not tested. There is, however, an option in Excel which will find any data that do not meet the criteria. (cf. below: Tracing unauthorised data).*

⇨ *The options on the **Input Message** page of the **Data - Validation** dialog box make it possible to display a message in a ScreenTip when the mouse pointer is on the cell. The options under the **Error Alert** tab allow you to enter a message to display when the data entered do not meet the validation criteria.*

F- Tracing unauthorised data

*This is a technique for finding cells whose values do not meet any validation criteria you may have set using the **Data - Validation** options. Cells containing invalid data are circled in red.*

▦ Show the **Formula Auditing** toolbar:

Tools - Formula Auditing - Show Formula Auditing Toolbar

▦ Click the ▦ tool button.

⇨ *To remove the red circles, click the ▦ tool button.*

9.2 Workgroups

A- Managing shared workbooks

Sharing a workbook

▦ **Tools - Share Workbook - Editing** tab

▦ Tick the **Allow changes by more than one user...** option then click **OK**.

▦ Confirm the message that offers to save the workbook.

Using a shared workbook

▦ Open the shared workbook.

*The term **[Shared]** on the title bar indicates that you are using a shared workbook.*

▦ Make your changes.

Some actions cannot be performed on shared workbooks. For example, you cannot merge cells, create charts or drawing objects, insert pictures or create subtotals or pivot tables.

▓ Save the shared workbook to update the changes made and saved by other users. If another user has saved changes to the shared workbook and there is no conflict in the changes made, the following message appears:

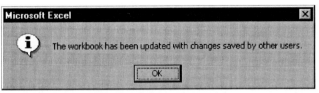

A coloured border appears around cells that have been modified by other users. If you point to one of these cells, a ScreenTip appears relating the details of the changes made, such as the author, date and time and the type of changes.

▓ If you want to know who currently is working on the shared workbook, use **Tools - Share Workbook** - **Editing** tab.

⇨ *If you would prefer other users' changes to be updated at regular intervals rather than each time the workbook is saved, go into **Tools - Share Workbook - Advanced** tab. In the **Update changes** frame, tick the **Automatically every** option and specify a time interval in minutes. This option can be modified independently by each user.*

Resolving modification conflicts

If you modify the same cells as another user and try to save those changes, a conflict occurs. Excel displays a dialog box that allows you to choose which changes are saved.

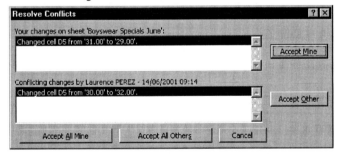

▓ To examine each conflicting change one by one, click **Accept Mine** or **Accept Other** to confirm respectively your own modification or that of the other user and go on to the next modification.

▓ To accept all your changes or all those made by the other user, click **Accept All Mine** or **Accept All Others** as required.

⇨ *If you wish to give your changes priority over those made by other users, which means that the **Resolve Conflicts** dialog box will no longer appear, activate the **The changes being saved win** option (**Tools - Share Workbook - Advanced** tab - **Conflicting changes between users** frame).*

Unsharing a workbook

- **Tools - Share Workbook - Editing** tab
- Deactivate the **Allow changes by more than one user** option.
- Click **Yes** on the dialog box that asks if you are sure you no longer want to share the workbook.

B-Merging workbooks

It is possible to make copies of a shared workbook, with each copy being modified by a different user independently. The copied workbooks, and their modifications, can then be merged into a single workbook.

Copying a shared workbook

- **Tools - Share Workbook - Editing** tab
- If the workbook is not yet shared, tick the **Allow changes by more than one user** option then click the **Advanced** tab.
- Check that the **Keep change history for** option is active in the **Track changes** frame.
- If necessary, modify the number of days during which the other users can change or add comments to the copies of the shared workbook.

  You will not be able to merge the copies of the workbook once this reviewing date is passed. If you are unsure about the amount of time required, enter a high number such as 1000 days.

- Click **OK**.
- If necessary, confirm saving the workbook.
- To make the copies of the workbook, use the **File - Save As** command and give each copy a different name.

Merging two or more workbooks

- Open the shared workbook in which you wish to merge the modifications made to all the copies.
- **Tools - Compare and Merge Workbooks**
- If necessary, confirm saving the workbook.
- In the **Select Files to Merge into Current Workbook** dialog box, select the copy or copies of the shared workbook whose changes you wish to merge.

  To select several files, use ⇧ Shift to select adjacent files or Ctrl to select nonadjacent ones.

- Click **OK** to start the merge.

C-Tracking changes

Tracking the changes in a shared workbook

▒ Open the shared workbook then use **Tools - Track Changes - Highlight Changes**.

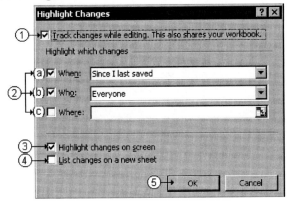

① Activate this option.

② Indicate the changes that you want to see highlighted:

(a)　Choose the time interval that interests you.

(b)　Choose the users whose changes should be highlighted.

(c)　Choose to highlight the changes in a specific range of cells.

If none of the three **Highlight which changes** options are active, Excel will pick out all the changes made by all the users of the shared workbook, including your own.

③ Tick this check box if you want Excel to mark the changes directly in the cells.

④ Choose this option to show all the changes as a list in a new sheet called **History**. This list can be filtered.

⑤ Click to confirm.

Accepting or rejecting changes in a shared workbook

▒ Open the shared workbook then use **Tools - Track Changes - Accept or Reject Changes**.

▒ If Excel offers to save the workbook, click **OK**.

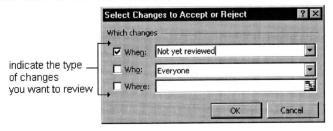

indicate the type of changes you want to review

MACROS

If none of these three options are active, Excel reviews all the changes made to the shared workbook.

▓ Click **OK**.

*The modification details appear in the **Accept or Reject Changes** dialog box and the first modification is highlighted in the workbook.*

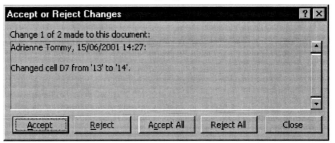

▓ To review the changes one at a time, choose to **Accept** or **Reject** with the appropriate buttons. Excel will go on to the next change.

If several changes have been made to the same cell, Excel will ask you to choose a value. If this happens, choose the correct value and click Accept.

▓ To act upon all the changes at once, use the buttons to **Accept All** the changes or **Reject All** of them.

D-Protecting a shared workbook

You should activate this protection before sharing the workbook.

▓ Open the workbook that is not currently shared then use **Tools - Protection - Protect and Share Workbook**.

▓ Tick the **Sharing with track changes** option.

▓ To prevent other users removing the protection, enter a **Password**.

▓ Click **OK** then enter the password again to confirm it and click **OK** again.

▓ Confirm saving the workbook.

*The workbook is shared automatically. The **Allow changes by more than one user** options under the **Editing** tab and the **Track changes** option under the **Advanced tab** (**Tools - Share Workbook**) are no longer available.*

⇨ *To remove the protection, and stop the workbook from being shared, use the **Tools - Protection - Unprotect Shared Workbook** command, enter the password if necessary and confirm the message that asks if you no longer wish to share the workbook.*

E-Sending a workbook for review

If you want one or more colleagues to review a workbook, you can send them a link to the workbook saved on a network or send them a copy of it. This command can be used only if you have Outlook 2002.

▨ Open the workbook you wish to send for review then use **File - Send To - Mail Recipient (for Review).**

▨ If the workbook you wish to send is saved on a network, a message appears asking if you would like to send a copy of the file as well as a link to it. Click **Yes** or **No** depending on what you require.

▨ If the workbook you wish to send is saved on your hard disk, Excel may prompt you to saved a shared version of the workbook. If you want to track changes or merge changes at a later time, click **Yes** and indicate where to save the copy, otherwise click **No.**

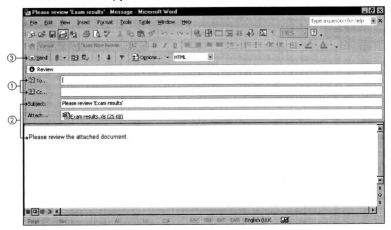

① Give the address(es) to which you are sending the workbook and also any to which you are sending a copy.

② If necessary, change the message subject and enter any further comments in the main message pane.

③ Click to send the message.

⇨ *The recipient receives a message containing (depending on the options chosen as you prepared it) an attached workbook file and/or a link to the file on a network. The recipient can make changes to the workbook and return it to the sender by using the* **File - Send To - Original Sender** *command. This message can be modified in the usual ways and sent using the* **Send** *button.*

MACROS

10.1 Smart Tags

A-What is a smart tag?

*Sometimes, when you have entered data into an Excel cell, a purple triangle may appear in the top corner of the cell. This indicator means that Excel has associated a **smart tag** with that cell.*

Smart tags can be used to perform certain actions usually performed by other applications within Excel. The actions proposed depend on the type of data that Excel recognises. For example :

E-mail recipients A user name such as Sandra Reid may be recognised by Excel as a "recent mail recipient" smart tag. The associated actions enable you to add that person's name and address in your Outlook 2002 contacts folder.

Financial symbols Other smart tags may appear; for example, if you enter a financial symbol into a cell, a smart tag will enable you to obtain information about that company, such as stock prices.

	A	B	C
1	**Airline Offices**		
2			
3	**Airline Name**	**Contact Person**	**Phone Number**
13	Alitalia	Marco Iezzi	131-856 9632
14	American Airlines	Andrew Blackburn	131-887 2323
15	Argentina Airways	Rebecca Tilsden	131-996 5213
16	BritAir	Richard Bray	131-887 4125
17	British Airways	Debbie Hanlon	131-856 4758

*In this example, a smart tag indicator has appeared next to the name **Andrew Blackburn** (as a recent e-mail recipient).*

You must activate the smart tag feature before you can use them.

B-Activating smart tags

▓ **Tools - AutoCorrect Options**

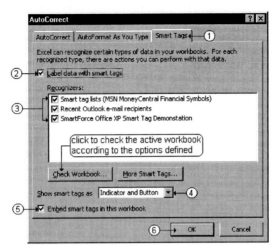

① Select this tab.

② Activate this option.

③ To choose what type of data Excel should recognise and label with smart tags, activate or deactivate these options.

④ Specify whether smart tags should be displayed with a cell indicator (the triangle in the corner) and/or the ⊙ ▾ button.

⑤ To save the smart tags when you save the workbook, activate this option.

⑥ Click to confirm.

C-Using smart tags

▓ Point to the smart tag indicator in the corner of the cell to make the **Smart Tag Actions** button ⊙ ▾ appear.

▓ Click the ⊙ ▾ button to see the list of actions associated with this type of data.

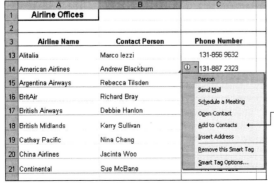

D-Downloading new smart tags

You can download new smart tags from Web sites to add to those already installed with the Microsoft Excel application. Other smart tags may be created by Microsoft but mainly by other IT companies and technicians.
New smart tags are being developed constantly so you can download new smart tags regularly, if you wish.

▨ **Tools - AutoCorrect Options - Smart Tags** tab

▨ Click the **More Smart Tags** option.

A page from the Microsoft Web site appears in your Web browser window, showing the categories into which the smart tags are organised.

▨ Click the link that corresponds to the category that interests you then click the link to download the required smart tag application.

E-Deleting smart tags

▨ To delete a smart tag, point to the cell until the **Smart Tag Actions** button appears, click the button and choose the **Remove this Smart Tag** option.

▨ To remove all the smart tags from the current workbook, deactivate the **Label text with smart tags** and the **Embed smart tags in this workbook** options in the **AutoCorrect Options** dialog box (**Tools - auto Correct Options, Smart Tags** tab).

▨ Click **OK**.

▨ Close then open the workbook again to make these changes take effect.

⇨ *You can deactivate specific types of smart tags by deactivating the corresponding option in the Recognizers list and the Embed smart tags in this workbook option. Save the workbook, close it then open it again.*

10.2 Importing data

A-Copying data from another application into Excel

▨ Open the application then the file in which the data you want to copy are stored.

▨ Select the data you want to copy.

If you are copying text that is not separated by a delimiter (for example, a tab stop), it will be pasted into a single cell in the Excel sheet.

▨ Copy the data, using the appropriate command. For Office applications, use **Edit - Copy** or ▨ or ⌷Ctrl⌷ **C**.

- Open the Excel application, if necessary, then the workbook in which you want to paste the copied data.
- Activate the first destination cell for the copy.
- To paste the data, without creating a link, use **Edit - Paste** or 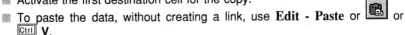 or `Ctrl` **V**.
- To paste data with a link, so any changes to the source data are carried over into the Excel worksheet, use **Edit - Paste Special**. Activate the **Paste link** option and in the **As** list, choose the format the pasted data should take then click **OK**.

B-Importing data from a Web page

Using a Web query

A Web query enables you to import data from a Web page, originating from one or more tables; this data can be updated.

- Activate a cell outside a range of imported data.
- **Data - Import External Data - New Web Query**

① Enter the URL of the Web page from which you wish to import data (a) or expand the list to choose a recently visited **Address** (b) then start the search (c).

② Click the ⬛➡ symbol to the top left of any frame(s) you wish to import or click the ⬛➡ symbol in the upper left corner of the page to import the data from the whole page.

The ⬛➡ symbol is transformed into ⬛✔.

③ Click this button to view and possibly modify the default options for formatting and importing Web data.

④ If you wish to be able to extract the query data into other workbooks or share the query with other users, you should save that query: click this tool button, select the file in which to save and enter the **File name** then click **Save**.

A Web query is saved as a file with an **.iqy** extension. If you do not save the Web query as a separate file, it will be saved as part of your workbook and can only be run from that workbook.

⑤ Start importing.

▨ In the **Import Data** dialog box, specify where to place the imported data then click **OK**.

The ⬤ icon appears briefly on the status bar, indicating that Excel is in the process of importing the data.

⇨ *You can modify the source of a Web query by activating one of the items of imported data then using the **Data - Import External Data - Edit Web Query** command or click ⬛ on the **External Data** toolbar.*

⇨ *To run a saved Web Query, use the **Data - Import External Data - Import Data** command. Find and select the query you wish to run, click the **Open** button then select the option that corresponds to where you wish to place the imported data. Click **OK** to finish.*

Copying data from a Web page

This method can be used to copy data using the Internet Explorer Web browser (4.1 or later).

▨ In the browser, select the data you wish to copy then use **Edit - Copy**.

▨ Go into Excel and activate the first destination cell for the copied data then use **Edit - Paste** or ⬛.

▨ To change the way Excel pastes the data, click the ⬛ icon at the bottom right of the range of pasted cells and choose to **Keep Source Formatting**, or to **Match Destination Formatting**. The **Create Refreshable Web Query** option will create a query based on the Web page from which you copied the data.

C-Updating imported data

After you have imported your data, you can update it from Excel and modify the update settings.

▨ To update the data, activate one of the cells containing imported data then use **Data - Refresh Data** or ⬛.

Depending on the type of data you are refreshing and the current update settings, Excel may ask you to select the source file or enter a password.

▨ To modify the update settings, o activate one of the cells containing imported data then use **Data - Import External Data - Data Range Properties** or ⬛ (on the **External Data** toolbar).

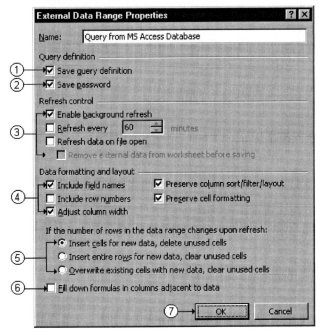

① Keep this option active if you want to be able to update the imported data.

② Choose this option enables to save a password entered once, so Excel does not ask for it each time you update the data.

③ Use these options to choose how Excel should update and how often.

④ Select formatting options for the imported data.

⑤ Indicate how Excel should react if the number of rows in the data range changes when you refresh the data.

⑥ Choose this option so that Excel will automatically copy any formulas that you may add after having imported the data.

⑦ Click to confirm.

10.3 Macros

A-Creating/deleting a macro

▓ If necessary, open the workbook concerned by the macro.

▓ **Tools - Macros - Record New Macro**

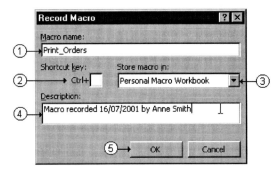

① Give the macro a name.

② If you wish, specify a shortcut key which will run the macro.

③ Indicate where the macro is to be stored: if you want the macro to be permanently accessible, choose **Personal Macro Workbook**.

④ If necessary, change the macro description.

⑤ Click to create the macro.

▓ Go through all the actions to be automated in the macro.

▓ When all the actions have been recorded, click the ▬ button on the **Stop Rec.** bar.

⇨ *Macros recorded in this way are created in a file called PERSONAL.XLS, where all personal macros are stored. This type of macro is always accessible as the PERSONAL workbook is automatically opened and hidden when Excel is started.*

⇨ *To delete a macro, use **Tools - Macro - Macros**, select the macro concerned then click **Delete** followed by **Yes** to confirm the deletion.*

B-Running a macro

▓ If a macro has been created in a workbook other than PERSONAL.XLS, open the workbook.

▓ **Tools - Macro - Macros** or [Alt] [F8]

▓ Double-click the macro you want to run.

⇨ *If the macro is stored in a workbook which is open or in PERSO-NAL.XLS, you can also run it by pressing the shortcut key defined when the macro was created.*

C-Loading an Add-In

These macros are provided with Excel but are not automatically loaded.

▓ **Tools - Add-Ins**

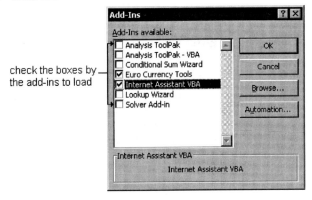

check the boxes by the add-ins to load

⇨ *Add-ins appear as options in different Excel menus.*

D-Viewing the contents of a macro

▓ If the macro is stored in PERSONAL.XLS, use the command **Window - Unhide** to display it, as you would for any other hidden workbook.

▓ **Tools - Macro - Macros** or [Alt] [F8]

▓ Select the macro, then click **Edit**.

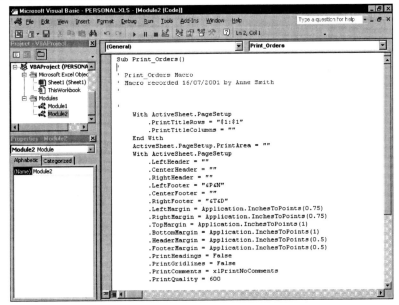

The contents of the macro, written in Visual Basic appear.

VARIOUS ADVANCED FEATURES

▬10.4 Creating a Web page

A-Accessing a Web server

Creating a shortcut to a folder on a Web server

If you want to publish your Web page in an existing folder on a Web server, you should create a shortcut to that folder before you start work.

▦ If necessary, open the task pane (**View - Task Pane**) and choose the **New Workbook** option.

▦ If you are working under Windows 2000 or Windows Me, click the **Add Network Place** link in the task pane then activate the **Create a shortcut to an existing Network Place** option in the **Add Network Place Wizard** dialog box.
If you are working under Windows NT 4.0 or Windows 98, click the **Add Web Folder** link in the task pane then activate the **Create a shortcut to an existing Web Folder** option.

▦ Click the **Next** button.

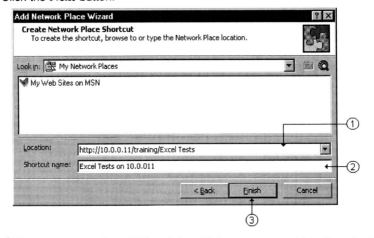

① Enter the complete URL of the Web server to which the shortcut should lead.

② If necessary, modify the shortcut name.

③ Click to confirm.

Creating a folder and its shortcut on a Web server

Before you publish a Web page on a Web server, you should first create a Web folder on the server as well as a shortcut to make it easier to access that folder.

▦ If necessary, display the **New Workbook** task pane.

▦ If you are working under Windows 2000 or Windows Me, click the **Add Network Place** link in the task pane then activate the **Create a new Network Place** option in the **Add Network Place Wizard** dialog box.

- If you are working under Windows NT 4.0 or Windows 98, click the **Add Web Folder** link in the task pane then activate the **Create a new Web Folder** option.
- Click the **Next** button.
- In the **Folder location** text box, enter the URL for the server on which you want to create the new folder (your administrator or ISP will have to supply you with the corresponding URL).
- Enter the **Folder name** for the folder you are creating.
- Click the **Next** button.
- Click the **Finish** button to create the new folder on the Web server and the corresponding shortcut in **My Network Places** (for Windows 2000 or Me) or **Network Neighborhood** (for Windows NT 4.0 or Windows 98).

B-Publishing a Web page

Publishing a non-interactive Web page

*A **non-interactive Web page** contains information that can be consulted by users visiting your Internet/intranet site but cannot be modified. You can publish a selection of cells, a worksheet or a whole Excel 2002 workbook as a non-interactive Web page.*

- Create or open the workbook (in xls or htm format) that you want to publish.
- If necessary, select the data you wish to publish, or if you want to publish a whole sheet or workbook, do not make any selection.
- **File - Save as Web Page**

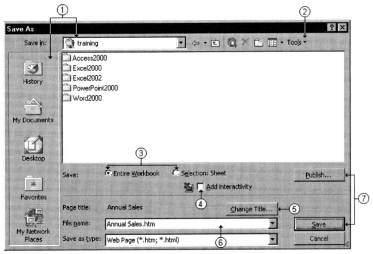

① Select the location in which you want to publish your Web page, using the **Save in** list and/or the **Places Bar**. Depending on your version of Windows, the **Places Bar** can take you rapidly to one of the previously created **Web Folders** (in Windows NT 4.0/98) or to the existing **My Network Places** (in Windows 2000/Me) (cf. previous sections).

② Use the **Web Options** in this menu to modify the settings for the Web page you are publishing: to choose a browser, a font, to manage published files and to specify encoding, etc.

③ Specify whether you are saving the entire workbook or just a selection.

④ Make sure that this option is not active.

⑤ If you wish, click this button and enter the text that will appear on the browser's title bar when the Web page is opened, then click **OK**.

⑥ If necessary, change the proposed name for the file.

⑦ To save the Web page, without accessing the publication options, click this button.

The Web page appears in htm format and the original file closes automatically. Along with the Web page, Excel generates a folder that contains all the components of the Web page, which are called "supporting files"; this separate folder appears only when you save, not publish, a Web page. This folder is called **[Web page name]_files**; the supporting files folder and the Web page are indissociable.

To publish your Web page, choosing more advanced options if you wish, click the **Publish** button.

A new dialog box appears:

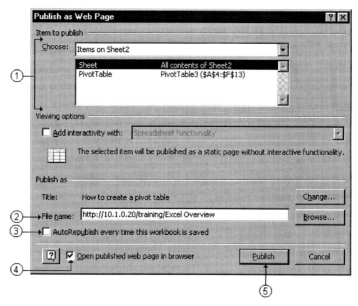

① Select the item you want to publish.

② If you are publishing the Web page on your own computer, modify this address (if necessary), making sure you use this syntax: *drive:\folder\file.htm*.

If you are publishing the Web page on a Web server, modify this address (if necessary), making sure you use this syntax: *http://server_address/file.htm (for example http://10.1.0.20/excel_training/pivot_tables.htm*.

③ Tick this check box if you want Excel to update the Web page each time you save changes to the source file.

④ To preview the Web page in the default browser once you have published it, make sure there is a tick in this check box.

⑤ Click this button.

If you chose to see a preview, the default browser opens and displays the Web page.

▓ Once you have finished checking your page, close the browser window.

⇨ *If you published your Web page on your own workstation, you can check the result by viewing the file in your Web browser. If necessary, modify the original workbook you used to create the Web page then when you are satisfied with the result, publish the Web page again using the same procedure but replace the address of your own computer by the address of the Web server concerned.*

⇨ *If you saved (not published) a whole workbook as a non-interactive Web page, you can still preview the page without publishing it. To do this, open the htm file in question then use the **Web Page Preview** command in the **File** menu.*

Publishing an interactive Web page

A visitor to an interactive Web page can modify the page, but he/she must have Internet Explorer (4.01 or later) installed on his/her computer and also have the appropriate Microsoft Office licence to use worksheets, charts and pivot table lists published exclusively from Microsoft Excel.

▓ Create or open the worksheet (in xls or htm format) that you want to publish.

▓ If you want to publish only one of the sheets in the workbook, click its tab to activate it.

▓ **File - Save As Web Page**

▓ Select the location in which you want to publish your Web page, using the **Save in** list or the **Places Bar**. Depending on your version of Windows, the **Places Bar** can take you rapidly to one of the previously created **Web Folders** (in Windows NT 4.0/98) or to the existing **My Network Places** (in Windows 2000/Me) (cf. previous sections).

▓ Use the **Web Options** in the **Tools** menu to modify the settings for the Web page you are publishing: to choose a browser, a font, to manage published files and to specify encoding, etc.

▓ Choose the **Entire Workbook** option to publish the whole workbook or the **Selection** option to publish the active sheet then tick the **Add Interactivity** check box.

VARIOUS ADVANCED FEATURES

▓ If necessary, click the **Change Title** button to enter the text that will appear in the browser's title bar when you open the Web page then click **OK**.

▓ If you wish, modify the suggested **File name**.

▓ To save the Web page, without accessing the publication options, click the **Save** button.

The Web page appears in htm format and the original file closes automatically. For an interactive Web page, Excel does not generate a supporting files folder.

▓ To publish your Web page, choosing more advanced options click the **Publish** button.

A new dialog box appears.

▓ In the **Choose** list, select the element you want to publish.

What appears in this list depends on the contents of the Web page.

▓ Make sure the **Add interactivity with** check box is still ticked and if necessary, open the attached drop-down list to choose which Excel functionality you want to make available to users of the page.
If you publish a whole workbook, the **Add interactivity with** option appears greyed-out, as it is unavailable.

▓ Click the **Change** button if you want to modify the name entered for the page during the previous step.

▓ By default the place of publication, followed by the file name defined in the previous step, appear in the **File name** text box.

▓ Tick the **AutoRepublish every time this workbook is saved** check box if you want Excel to update the Web page each time you save changes to the source file.

▓ To preview the Web page in the default browser once you have published it, make sure there is a tick in the **Open published web page in browser** check box.

▓ Click the **Publish** button.

If you are publishing a pivot table, your browser may inform you that the source data for your table is located in another domain.

▓ In this case, click **Yes** to continue.

Here is an example of a published interactive worksheet:

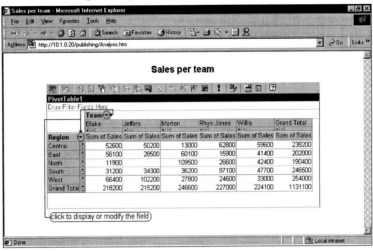

Here is an example of a published interactive workbook:

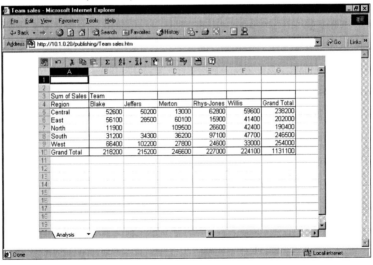

You can see that the network user cannot work with the pivot table in the same way as with the previous example. Here, some of the fields are inactive, there are less tools available and so on.

░ When you have finished your work, close the browser window.

░ If you wish, close the Excel file.

⇨ *To delete a Web page, use the Windows Explorer to go to the server and/or folder where the Web page is located. Select the Web page ([filename].htm) and its supporting files folder ([filename]_files), if you are deleting a saved (not published) non-interactive Web page. Press the* Del *key and click* Yes *to confirm the file deletion.*

WORKING WITH MENUS AND OPTIONS

Display shortcut menu   `⇧ Shift` `F10`

File

New	`Ctrl` **N**	Save As	`F12`
Open	`Ctrl` **O**	Print	`Ctrl` **P**
Save	`Ctrl` **S**	Exit	`Alt` `F 4`

Edit

Undo	`Ctrl` **Z**	Clear contents	`Del`
Repeat	`Ctrl` **Y**	Delete	`Ctrl` **-**
Cut	`Ctrl` **X**	Find	`Ctrl` **F**
Copy	`Ctrl` **C**	Find next	`⇧ Shift` `F 4`
Paste	`Ctrl` **V**	Find previous	`Ctrl` `⇧ Shift` `F 4`
Fill down	`Ctrl` **D**	Replace	`Ctrl` **H**
Fill right	`Ctrl` **R**	Go To	`F 5` or `Ctrl` **G**

Insert

Cells, Rows, Columns	`Ctrl` **+ (numbercpad)**		
Worksheet	`⇧ Shift` `F 11`	Name	
Chart		Define	`Ctrl` `F3`
As New Sheet	`F 11`	Paste	`F3`
		Create	`Ctrl` `⇧ Shift` `F 3`
Cell comment	`⇧ Shift` `F 2`	Hyperlink	`Ctrl` **K**

Format

Cells, Object	`Ctrl` **1**	Column	
Row		Hide	`Ctrl` **0**
Hide	`Ctrl` **9**	Unhide	`Ctrl` `⇧ Shift` **0**
Unhide	`Ctrl` `⇧ Shift` **9**	Style	`Alt` **'**

Tools

Spelling	`F7`	Calculation	
Macro		Calculate Now	`F9`
Macros	`Alt` `F 8`	Calculate worksheet	`⇧ Shift` `F 9`
Visual Basic Editor	`Alt` `F 11`		
Microsoft Script Editor	`Alt` `⇧ Shift` `F 4`		

Data

Group and Outline	
Group	`Alt` `⇧ Shift` `→`
Ungroup	`Alt` `⇧ Shift` `←`

Help

Microsoft Excel Help	`F1`
What's This?	`⇧ Shift` `F 1`

OTHER KEY COMBINATIONS

Entering data

Enter the current date	`Ctrl` ;
Enter the current time	`Ctrl` `⇧ Shift` :
Euro symbol	`Alt Gr` 4
Insert same formula/ value as cell above	`Ctrl` '

Insert value only from cell above	`Ctrl` `⇧ Shift` "
Insert Autosum	`Alt` =
Clear selection of formulas/data	`Del`
Tab within a text box	`Ctrl` `⇄`

Working in the Formula Bar

Activate Edit mode in cell and formula bar	`F2`
Start a formula	=
Delete from insertion point to the end of line	`Ctrl` `Del`
Insert a line break	`Alt` `Enter`
Cancel unconfirmed entry	`Esc`
Confirm cell entry	`Enter`

Confirm an array formula	`Ctrl` `⇧ Shift` `Enter`
Fill selected range with the current entry	`Ctrl` `Enter`
Create relative/ absolute references	`F4`
After a function has been entered, displays the formula palette	`Ctrl` A
After a function has been entered, displays function arguments	`Ctrl` `⇧ Shift` A

Formatting cells

Apply an outline border	`Ctrl` `⇧ Shift` &
Remove all borders	`Ctrl` `⇧ Shift` -
Apply or remove bold type	`Ctrl` B

Apply or remove italics	`Ctrl` I
Apply or remove an underline	`Ctrl` U

Formatting numbers and dates

Apply General format	`Ctrl` `⇧ Shift` ~
Apply Comma format	`Ctrl` `⇧ Shift` !
Apply dd/mmm/yy Date format	`Ctrl` #

Currency format, two decimal places	`Ctrl` `⇧ Shift` $
Exponential number format, two decimal places	`Ctrl` `⇧ Shift` ^

Moving in worksheets

Beginning of current row	`↖`
A1 on current sheet	`Ctrl` `↖`
Final cell in the range you worked in	`Ctrl` `End`
Next window	`Ctrl` `F6` or `Ctrl` `⇄`
Previous window	`Ctrl` `⇧ Shift` `F6` or `Ctrl` `⇧ Shift` `⇄`

Next sheet in the workbook	`Ctrl` `Pg Dn`
Previous sheet in the workbook	`Ctrl` `Pg Up`
Next pane in a split worksheet	`F6`
Previous pane in a split worksheet	`⇧ Shift` `F6`

Selecting

Whole sheet	`Ctrl` A
Whole column	`Ctrl` `space`
Whole row	`⇧ Shift` `space`

Activates/deactivates extend mode	`F 8`
Add a range of cells to current selection	`⇧ Shift` `F 8`

Selecting of individual cells

Cells containing comments	`Ctrl` `⇧ Shift` O
Rectangular range of cells surrounding the active cell	`Ctrl` `⇧ Shift` *
The entire array to which the cell belongs	`Ctrl` /
Only cells to which the formulas in the selection make direct reference.	`Ctrl` [
All cells to which formulas in the selection make direct or indirect reference.	`Ctrl` `⇧ Shift` [
Only cells with formulas that refer directly to the active cell.	`Ctrl`]
All cells with formulas that refer directly or indirectly to the active cell.	`Ctrl` `⇧ Shift`]
Only visible cells in the current selection.	`Alt` ;
Select cells in a selected row whose contents are different from the active cell.	`Ctrl` \
Select cells in a selected column whose contents are different from the comparison cell in each column	`Ctrl` `⇧ Shift` /

Outline view

Group rows or columns	`Alt` `⇧ Shift` `→`
Ungroup rows or columns	`Alt` `⇧ Shift` `←`
Show/hide outline symbols	`Ctrl` 8

Standard Toolbar

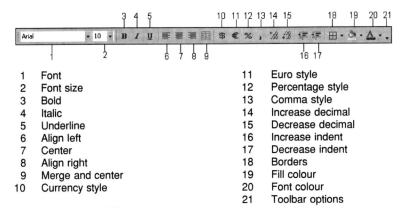

1	New workbook	13	Undo
2	Open	14	Redo
3	Save	15	Insert hyperlink
4	E-mail	16	AutoSum
5	Search (task pane)	17	Euro conversion
6	Print	18	Sort ascending
7	Print preview	19	Sort descending
8	Spelling	20	Chart Wizard
9	Cut	21	Drawing
10	Copy	22	Zoom
11	Paste	23	Microsoft Excel help
12	Format painter		

Formatting Toolbar

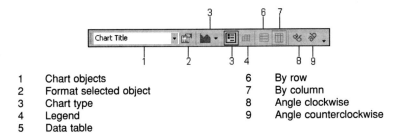

1	Font	11	Euro style
2	Font size	12	Percentage style
3	Bold	13	Comma style
4	Italic	14	Increase decimal
5	Underline	15	Decrease decimal
6	Align left	16	Increase indent
7	Center	17	Decrease indent
8	Align right	18	Borders
9	Merge and center	19	Fill colour
10	Currency style	20	Font colour
		21	Toolbar options

N.B.: A Euro tool **€** appears on this toolbar when the **Euro Currency Tools** add-in is installed.

Chart Toolbar

1	Chart objects	6	By row
2	Format selected object	7	By column
3	Chart type	8	Angle clockwise
4	Legend	9	Angle counterclockwise
5	Data table		

Microsoft Excel 2002

Drawing Toolbar

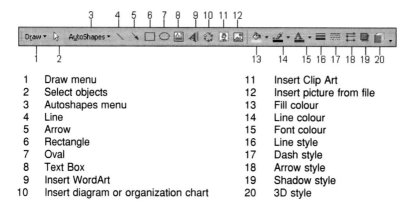

1	Draw menu	11	Insert Clip Art
2	Select objects	12	Insert picture from file
3	Autoshapes menu	13	Fill colour
4	Line	14	Line colour
5	Arrow	15	Font colour
6	Rectangle	16	Line style
7	Oval	17	Dash style
8	Text Box	18	Arrow style
9	Insert WordArt	19	Shadow style
10	Insert diagram or organization chart	20	3D style

Reviewing Toolbar

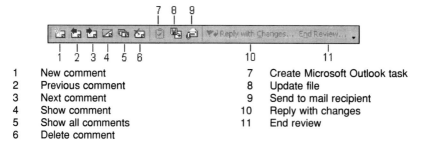

1	New comment	7	Create Microsoft Outlook task
2	Previous comment	8	Update file
3	Next comment	9	Send to mail recipient
4	Show comment	10	Reply with changes
5	Show all comments	11	End review
6	Delete comment		

Formula Auditing Toolbar

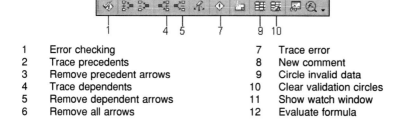

1	Error checking	7	Trace error
2	Trace precedents	8	New comment
3	Remove precedent arrows	9	Circle invalid data
4	Trace dependents	10	Clear validation circles
5	Remove dependent arrows	11	Show watch window
6	Remove all arrows	12	Evaluate formula

Picture Toolbar

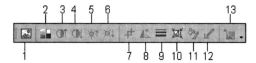

1	Insert picture from file	7	Crop
2	Color	8	Rotate left
3	More contrast	9	Line style
4	Less contrast	10	Compress pictures
5	More brightness	11	Format object
6	Less brightness	12	Set transparent colour
		13	Reset picture

PivotTable Toolbar

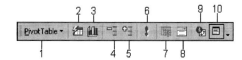

1	PivotTable menu	6	Refresh data
2	Format report	7	Include hidden items in totals
3	Chart Wizard	8	Always display items
4	Hide detail	9	Field settings
5	Show detail	10	Show field list

WordArt Toolbar

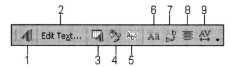

1	Insert WordArt	6	WordArt same letter heights
2	Edit text	7	WordArt vertical text
3	WordArt gallery	8	WordArt alignment
4	Format WordArt	9	WordArt character spacing
5	WordArt shape		

D

DATA

DATA CATEGORIES

DATA LISTS

DATA SERIES

INDEX

INDEX

Microsoft Excel 2002

ZOOMING